Word in Flower:
The Visualization of Classical Literature in Seventeenth-Century Japan

Edited by Carolyn Wheelwright

Yale University Art Gallery   New Haven   Connecticut

This catalogue accompanies an
exhibition held at Yale University Art Gallery
between 22 September and 12 November 1989

Publication of this catalogue
was subsidized by a grant from the
Mary Livingston Griggs and Mary Griggs Burke Foundation.

Copyright © 1989 by Yale University Art Gallery
All rights reserved.
Library of Congress Catalogue Card Number:89–51369
International Standard Book Number: ISBN 0-89467-051-4

Printed in U.S.A.

Contents

5   Director's Foreword   Mary Gardner Neill

7   Curator's Preface   James T. Ulak

9   Lenders to the Exhibition

12 Introduction   Carolyn Wheelwright

16 The Past in the Present: Edward Kamens
    Fujiwara Teika and the Traditions
    of Japanese Poetry

28 Translation of Teika's Poems   Edward Kamens
    on *Flowers and Birds of the Twelve Months*

33 Re-Presenting Teika's *Flowers and Birds*   Kendall Brown

54 Images of the *Tales of Ise*   Helen Mitsu Nagata

84 Past and Present, Text and Image   Carolyn Wheelwright

109 Catalogue

118 Japanese Historical Periods

118 Map of Central Japan:
    Important Sites in *The Tales of Ise*

119 Selected Bibliography

122 Index

Fig. 1. Black lacquer sake bottles with gold design of *Bamboo and Snow* (Cat. 14).

Director's Foreword

Earlier in this century, the novelist Jun'ichiro Tanizaki, in his evocative essay entitled "In Praise of Shadows," noted that "the quality we call beauty... must always grow from the realities of life." Western audiences, generally undeterred by language and other cultural barriers, have demonstrated an increasing attraction to Japanese art. "Word in Flower: The Visualization of Classical Literature in Seventeenth-Century Japan" offers an array of complex pleasures and a delightfully encoded world of refined sensibilities. It examines a rapidly evolving Japanese society that found stability and creative energy in the artistic reconstruction of a classical tradition. The exhibition, with its accompanying publication, explores the intriguing interaction of word and image, greatly enhancing our potential to grasp an art of considerable beauty and intellectual subtlety.

The Yale University Art Gallery prides itself on offering access to the resources of a great educational institution, particularly the expertise of scholars in multiple disciplines. This project, organized by Carolyn Wheelwright (Associate Professor of History of Art), Edward Kamens (Assistant Professor of Japanese Literature), and James Ulak (Associate Curator of Asian Art), exemplifies interdisciplinary collaboration. We are indebted to them for their love of Japan, mastery of their respective disciplines, and commitment to their students who helped to explore the ideas and select the objects presented in the catalogue and exhibition.

Exhibitions, especially those involving numerous loans and accompanied by illustrated catalogues, are expensive. This one would not have been possible without grants from the Japan Foundation, through its Art Exhibition Assistance Program, and from the Ishibashi Foundation. They have generously demonstrated Japanese confidence in our efforts to tell this story of their nation's artistic heritage. We are also indebted to the generous support of the Patrons of Yale University Art Gallery.

The handsome and informative catalogue was made possible by the Mary Livingston Griggs and Mary Griggs Burke Foundation, with a grant honoring C. E. Bayliss Griggs (Yale '39). Fifty remarkable years have passed since Mr. Griggs graduated from this institution. In that time, Japan has presented a face concurrently beguiling, fierce, challenging, and always complex. We hope that this exhibition, in its attention to beautiful particulars, will reveal to the careful viewer a profoundly human face.

Mary Gardner Neill
The Henry J. Heinz II Director

Fig. 2. Yamamoto Soken. *Teika's Poems on Flowers and Birds of the Twelve Months*, detail of the seventh month (Cat. 6).

Curator's Preface

"Word in Flower" grew from the close study of a single work in the Yale Collection, Teika's *Poems on Flowers and Birds of the Twelve Months*. On this pair of screens, probably produced in the early 1690s, twelve court calligraphers and the painter Yamamoto Soken interpreted twenty-four seasonal poems composed in 1214 by Fujiwara Teika. In the seventeenth century, creative retrieval of a "normative" past became an experience available to increasingly broader segments of society and was explored in virtually all media. These screens exemplify a consuming interest in producing sparkling, sensitive, allusive works formed by a subtle blend of talents. Delight, sustenance, and creative advance became the rewards of giving voice to the past.

"Word in Flower" is about words and images. Most often, the words are old, and when visible, they are in themselves both word and picture: calligraphed ideograms, "picture words" placed in action with the painted image. These combinations are fascinating and invariably fruitful. "Word in Flower" is also about invisible words imbedded in images, about texts so thoroughly absorbed by a literate culture that the textured surface of a tea bowl or a single fallen petal rendered in opaque pigment can become both generally evocative of and specifically referential to a classical source. The "flowering of word" is also about sheer, and not always sophisticated, proliferation: the dissemination of a newly agreed upon canon to an increasingly literate audience.

Preparing the exhibition has been, at every stage, a collaboration between Yale's academic and museum professionals. Our hope was to mount an exhibition in which familiar works would be balanced with those less well known; our aim was to present all in a fresh and thought-provoking context. American collections of Japanese art are particularly rich in the fruits of this seventeenth-century Japanese renaissance. When we tentatively approached lenders, institutional and private, and expressed our interest in studying the manifestations and implications of the neoclassicizing phenomenon, the response was enthusiastic. We are deeply grateful to all of them for their generous endorsement of and participation in this project. We are especially appreciative of the tolerance shown by collectors who had the dubious advantage of being nearby. They were always gracious hosts to our too frequent forays from New Haven.

The organic nature of the art we study confounds certain modern disciplinary divisions: the project has been, of necessity, interdisciplinary. As curator of the exhibition, my debt to and admiration for Carolyn Wheelwright and Edward Kamens, is immense. Professor Wheelwright, senior member of the exhibition team, generously offered her considerable pedagogic and research talents as general editor of this catalogue. She has been a mainstay throughout, rallying flagging spirits and refocusing diverted attention with energy and dedication. Professor Kamens infused our endeavor with his essential knowledge of "the word." His erudition, sensitivity to language, and poet's ear have enriched all aspects of this exhibition. Essays by graduate students Kendall Brown and Helen Mitsu Nagata are carefully honed and insightful contributions to our theme. Their work bodes well for the field of Japanese art history. Their presence at Yale has been rewarding to us all.

Noriko Yamamura, an independent scholar of medieval Japanese literature, cheerfully rescued us from various linguistic follies and regularly clarified indecipherable calligraphy with remarkable speed. Her painstaking transcription and identification of previously unstudied works enabled us to be confident in our presentation of the poems on three pairs of calligraphy screens: catalogue numbers 46, 47, and 48. Edwin Cranston of Harvard graciously read a draft of this work and offered important corrections and useful suggestions.

Greer Allen has produced a superb catalogue design: observing his passion for the elegant presentation of word and image gave us an uncanny sense of proximity to the concerns of his seventeenth-century counterparts. Barbara Folsom, diplomat and editor, patiently untangled garbled syntax, coaxed us to clarity, and wisely allowed the ambiguous its proper place. Charles Altschul's inventive and sensitive graphic designs have given an inviting public face to the exhibition.

The patience, good humor, and professionalism of the Art Gallery staff removed many obstacles on the long road from conception to installation. Mary Gardner Neill, whose support and encouragement has been constant, initially proposed the exhibition. The Yamamoto Soken screens, her prescient selection for acquisition, have been our primary inspiration. In all matters financial, from grant-writing advice to interpretation of arcane accounting language, Louisa Cunningham and Carolyn Giovanelli have graciously simplified our task. Susan Frankenbach, Diane Hart, and Lisa Davis of the Registrar's Office efficiently coordinated a mass of essential details. They were unflappable in the face of change and exemplary in their attention to the well-being of works of art. Richard Moore, Robert Soule, Jr., Michael Stack, and Cayse Cheatham handled every aspect of the physical installation with aplomb and skill. Experienced jugglers of contingencies, they crafted a handsome setting for the art. The installation design owes much to the efforts of graduate student Edward Douglas.

When several major projects vied for the attention of the Asian Art department, Melissa Thompson masterfully coordinated administrative details, structured schedules, and gave valued advice, which has enhanced both the form and content of the exhibition. Summer intern Eva Nagase cross-checked numerous references and enlightened us on many aspects of ceramic art.

As is demonstrated by the works illustrated in this catalogue, Japanese art of the highest quality is readily accessible in Western collections. We hope that this exhibition and its presentation will suggest rewarding avenues of exploration.

James T. Ulak
Associate Curator of Asian Art

Lenders to the Exhibition

The Art Institute of Chicago

Beinecke Rare Book and Manuscript Collection, Yale University

The Mary and Jackson Burke Collection

The Mary and Jackson Burke Foundation

The Cleveland Museum of Art

Peggy and Richard M. Danziger

The Harvard University Art Museums (Arthur M. Sackler Museum)

Mr. and Mrs. Leighton R. Longhi

Los Angeles County Museum of Art

The Metropolitan Museum of Art, New York

The Minneapolis Institute of Arts

Museum of Fine Arts, Boston

The Nelson-Atkins Museum of Art, Kansas City, Missouri

Salmon Collection

Seattle Art Museum

Spencer Collection, New York Public Library

Tiger Collection

Virginia Museum of Fine Arts

Yale University Art Gallery

Fig. 3. Overleaf. Attributed to Konoe Nobuhiro. *Spring Azaleas and Autumn Rushes*, detail (Cat. 46).

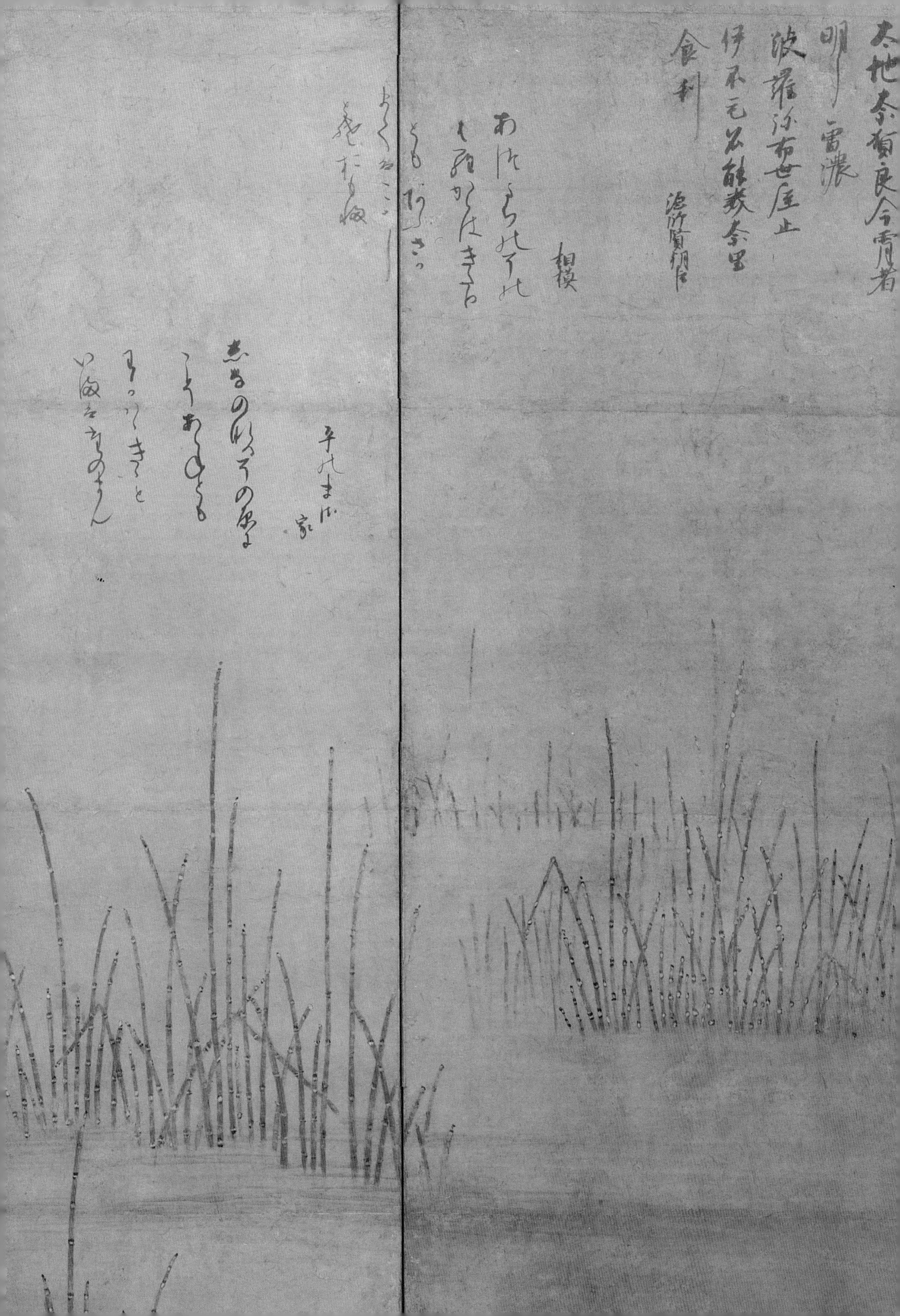

大地奈賀良今電者
明〳〵雷濃
波羅弥布世屋止
伊不元毛酔数奈里
食利
　　源所貨門佐

　　相摸
あれもちれも
も知ちにきち
ともちに
よく

　　平れまは家
志者のれうその手よ
うあきる
よつてきて
山海さきのうん

よくみに
花たる海

Introduction

Carolyn Wheelwright

> Japanese poetry has its seed in the human heart and finds expression in myriad leaves of words.
>
> Ki no Tsurayuki (ca. 872–945)
> *Kokinshū*, Japanese Preface

"Word in Flower" draws attention to the interaction between text and image in seventeenth-century Japanese art. While the close relationship of poetry, calligraphy, and painting characterizes much of Asian artistic expression, a particularly elegant union of the arts began to develop in the imperial capital of Kyoto during the final quarter of the sixteenth century. As more than a century of civil war climaxed in precipitous moves toward national unification, interest in the heritage of classical Japanese literature and the culture of the imperial court increased. Courtiers, impoverished by the disorders of the fifteenth and sixteenth centuries, exchanged their knowledge of the arts for sustenance, teaching courtly accomplishments to the newly risen warriors and the growing numbers of monied townsmen. The literary secrets of court poetry and romantic narrative, once the guarded preserve of the court, gradually were released into a larger cross section of society, while major court productions of calligraphy and paintings were dispersed, inspiring emulation. By the opening years of the seventeenth century, a remarkable artistic alliance of disenfranchised imperial aristocracy and wealthy but powerless commoners had formed. The aesthetic of the imperial court was about to become the property of a much larger public.

The primary referent for classical interests in the early seventeenth century was the canon of literature assembled in the early thirteenth century by Retired Emperor Gotoba and a coterie of brilliant court poets, chief among them Fujiwara Teika. Gotoba and his group anthologized, edited, and interpreted selected aristocratic verse and narrative of the preceding four centuries, adding significantly to that corpus. They explored anew the implications of a view of Japanese poetics as essentially lyrical. Thus Ki no Tsurayuki's early-tenth-century assertion that, "Japanese poetry has its seed in the human heart and finds expression in myriad leaves of words," itself experienced a new florescence among the circle of poets around Gotoba. Their legacy of "neoclassical" literature embodied the ideal of a courtly elite; their theories of poetics encouraged a regenerative approach to tradition.

Seventeenth-century literary men, courtier and commoner alike, looked to the poetic practice of Gotoba's era for inspiration and practical models. As Edward Kamens explains in his essay, "The Past in the Present," they overlooked the changes of time to assure that the present would remain in constant and direct contact with the past, for they viewed the traditions of Japanese poetry as the ultimate repository of human experience. They saw themselves as the direct inheritors of a literary tradition that had its most eloquent authority in Fujiwara Teika. Thus, they valued Teika's poetry, assimilated his poetic theories, accepted as definitive his scholarship on the Heian classics, treasured and emulated his idiosyncratic calligraphy. Most importantly, they adopted the central aesthetic dictum of his day, "Let the words be old ones and the sentiments new." Central to their method was continual reference to a canon of literature from which fragments could be abstracted and fused into a fresh expression. Like Teika, they sought to make use of the living literary past to capture the depth of experience of their present.

Seventeenth-century artists and craftsmen, like contemporary scholars and poets, demonstrated concern with heightening the experience of art by allusion to a shared tradition. They were sensitive to classical literary themes and the visual styles traditionally used to express them, but their continuity with the past was not restricted to simple illustration of classical literature. For these artists, as for Teika and other members of Gotoba's circle, visibility was already a central feature of poetry: verse was a thing to be seen, whether written in a courtier-poet's personalized calligraphy or conceived as a meaningful design element in a larger painting. Similarly, the ground on which text was written was seldom neutral, and traditions of decorated paper carried their own reserves of meaning. Both the awareness of the visible word and the message of nonfigural ornament mediate between the usual dichotomy of text and image, encouraging a fusion of the arts that conveys more intense expression. The best craftsmen, designers, painters, and calligraphers of the seventeenth century, as of Teika's time, were sensitive to the interdependence of word and image in artistic creation; their works reflect their attention to the meaning of the literary text, its visualization in calligraphy, its interpretation in painting, its expression in decoration and ornament.

The "Word in Flower" exhibition presents three complementary groupings of seventeenth-century art that incorporate, illustrate, and interpret literary themes associated with Fujiwara Teika and his thirteenth-century courtly environment. First is the art generated from Teika's twenty-four *Poems on Flowers and Birds of the Twelve Months*, composed in 1214 for screen paintings in the residence of one of Gotoba's sons (see below, pp. 27–28). Although nothing is known about the paintings, it was common practice in court circles from the ninth through the twelfth centuries for poems to be written about motifs featured in completed paintings. In other words, the painting came first, the poetry followed.

In the latter half of the seventeenth century, the procedure was just the reverse: artists of different studios used Teika's set of twenty-four poems as the basis for paintings. In "Re-Presenting Teika's *Flowers and Birds*," Kendall Brown examines several visualizations of this theme in the "Word in Flower" exhibition, relating each to established conventions of theme and motif in *yamato-e*, the traditional style of the imperial court. While all examples refer to the same verbal text, the visual images differ. The differences issue from the choice of format, the context of the flower and bird motifs, the sources of the motifs, the features of the painting style, the relationship of the written text to the painting, and numerous other components, such as the presence of painted decoration on poetry sheets or the use of silver leaf to portray glistening mists. One version presents the sequence of motifs in a narrative context, creating a "storybook classicism" (Fig. 15; Cat. 5); another echoes the format of traditional poet portraits, appropriating their iconic aura (Fig. 13); a third uses the natural motifs metaphorically to follow the progress of love (Fig. 16; Cat. 6). Each work of art establishes its own unique interaction between the poetic text and the visual images, whether they be painted, printed, decorated, or written.

The second part of "Word in Flower" deals with images of the *Tales of Ise*, a poetic narrative compiled in the tenth century, and popularly viewed as recounting the love adventures and lyric reflections of a ninth-century courtier-poet, Ariwara Narihira. By the early thirteenth century, several distinct textual versions of the classic existed. Fujiwara Teika, through extensive copying, collation, and commentary on the poetic episodes over a period of more than three decades, established the definitive version of the *Tales of Ise*, assuring its centrality in the classical canon. It was Teika's version of the *Ise* that provided the text for one of the first Saga-bon: luxury editions of the classics published in Saga, on the northwest edge of Kyoto, by Suminokura Soan in collaboration with Hon'ami Kōetsu. Printed on thick, tinted paper in moveable type, and interspersed with forty-nine illustrations, the 1608 Saga-bon *Ise* is a monument to the integrated courtly aesthetic shared by the circle of courtiers and elite townsmen of the Kyoto region (Fig. 29; Cat. 17).

As Helen Mitsu Nagata points out in her essay on "Images of the *Tales of Ise*," the widespread textual and visual knowledge promoted by the printed Saga-bon *Ise* had divergent effects on seventeenth-century pictorializations of the classic, suggesting two ways in which artists sought to bring the classical past into the present. While more conservative works preserve the past through close reproduction of traditional text and illustration as represented by the Saga-bon *Ise*, more creative images recall the past through new visual interpretations. Quickly identifiable motifs could be adapted to a wide range of illustrative formats; they could be embellished to add the excitement of modern society or reduced to essentials to allow more innovative formal treatment on album leaves or folding screens.

Moreover, episodes of the *Tales of Ise* are closely related to the *yamato-e* category of *meisho-e*, or "famous-place painting." When Narihira visited Yatsuhashi (Cat. 18a, 22a), the Sumiyoshi Shrine (Cat. 24d), or Musashi Plain (Cat. 31), he was stimulated to compose poetry in which the vocabulary of na-

ture expressed his human emotions. Once invested with the lyrical aura of Japanese *waka*, the locale became a famous place to be exalted in further poetry and recorded in scenic paintings. By the seventeenth century, artists could draw on centuries of traditional *meisho-e* associated with locales in the *Ise* episodes. Visual quotations from earlier compositions that allude to the literary histories of places bring meanings from those contexts, impressionistically layering them with the *Ise* motifs to create nuanced personal interpretations.

The third group of seventeenth-century objects in the "Word in Flower" exhibition focuses, literally, on words and flowers. In large-scale folding screens, as well as in small-scale decorated poetry-painting handscrolls and poetry sheets, these works capture the emotions of court poetry in visual language frequently interwoven with calligraphy, the visible word. Spanning the seventeenth century, this group of objects provides a visual and conceptual survey of the early-Edo-period response to classical literature and the courtly aesthetic.

As discussed in the concluding essay, "Past and Present, Text and Image," the central figure in the seventeenth-century renaissance of courtly taste was Hon'ami Kōetsu: calligrapher, potter, paper decorator, lacquer designer, tea master, and respected associate of Kyoto courtiers as well as elite townsmen. Kōetsu was the key participant in two collaborative projects that took place during the first decade of the seventeenth century and are emblematic of the renaissance of the courtly aesthetic: the publication of Japanese classical literature in the luxurious Saga-bon, already mentioned, and the production of poetry-painting scrolls and poetry sheets in association with Tawaraya Sōtatsu (Figs. 47, 4, and 52; Cat. 34, 39–40). In both cases, commonality of aesthetic taste resulted in remarkable integration of materials, technique, design, and artistic effect. The extended creative process of collaborative ventures, in which each craftsman contributed his part with the expectation that another would modify it with complementary techniques, led to a willingness to view a work of art as an organic visual process. Compositions that might have seemed incomplete before became lyrical glimpses of nature. Clusters of familiar autumn grasses shown near and distant convey a poetic attitude toward the season (Fig. 56; Cat. 44); botanically descriptive poppies in a striking expanse of flat gold leaf evoke admiration for the new and up-to-date (Fig. 57; Cat. 45).

"Word in Flower" calls attention to the translation of verbal literature into visual art. It implies transformation, as the word germinates and blossoms into something different from its original form. It also suggests interaction. In the early decades of the seventeenth century, a sense of communion with court art and a perception of unmediated contact with court poetry stimulated works in

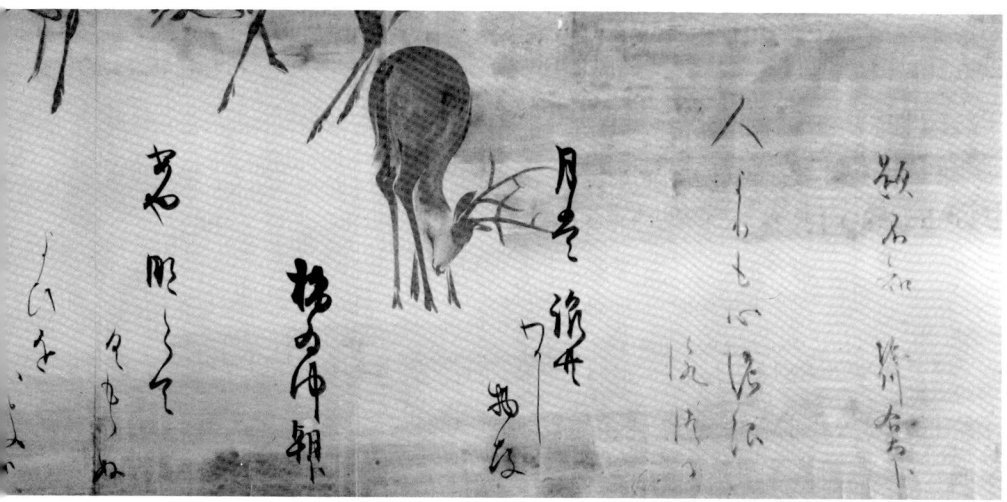

Fig. 4. Calligraphy by Hon'ami Kōetsu, painting by Tawaraya Sōtatsu. *Deer Scroll*, section (Cat. 39).

which referential images and allusive texts resound with new interpretations. When Kōetsu wrote a melancholy autumn poem on a poetry sheet decorated with silver cherry blossoms, he fused his expressive calligraphy with the flowers, transforming the thirteenth-century poem into a nuanced expression of seventeenth-century mutability (Fig. 47; Cat. 34). Motifs and styles, words and phrases abstracted from the past were placed in juxtaposition, resulting in a dense union full of the sense of the present. Nowhere is the dictum of Teika's circle more in evidence: "Let the words be old ones and the sentiments new."

Gradually the creative tensions that merged text and image in the early decades of the seventeenth century relaxed, to be replaced by more descriptive alignments of word and flower. Lovely poetry-painting scrolls and poetry sheets by followers of Kōetsu are fashionably elegant (Figs. 53–54; Cat. 41–42); screen paintings of poem slips tied to branches of blossoming trees entertain with the implied narrative of a recent blossom-viewing poem-writing party (Figs. 59–60; Cat. 47-48).

In the final decades of the seventeenth century, the conversion of word into flower was often lucidly structured. In the Yale screens by Yamamoto Soken, Teika's *Poems on Flowers and Birds of the Twelve Months* are matched with their visual counterparts, arrayed in clear compositional units (Fig. 16). Paired poetry sheets, decorated with gold underpainting and clouds of scattered bits of gold leaf, provide a traditional ground for the poems, which have been written in a mixture of Japanese phonetic script and Chinese characters in staggered lines of princely calligraphy. Beneath the poetry sheets, the celebrated flowers and birds are painted in clear colors on white silk, its surface enhanced with mists of silver leaf. The painter, the paper decorator, the twelve calligraphers of the imperial court, all participated in achieving a spacious balance of visual and verbal allusions to a courtly aesthetic that had become part of their sophisticated present.

During the course of the seventeenth century, the townsmen of Kyoto appropriated the heritage of the imperial court. Allied with cultivated courtiers who considered themselves guardians of the arts, they selectively drew on the long courtly tradition to create their own painting and calligraphy, lacquer and ceramics, textiles and printed books. Throughout the century, artists and craftsmen modified the art of the courtier to enhance the life of the merchant townsman. The rarefied aristocratic arts of the courtly past, thus transformed, fused into the mercantile context of the wealthy urban commoner, creating the particular kind of stylish elegance that still lingers in the ancient imperial capital.

The Past in the Present: Fujiwara Teika and the Traditions of Japanese Poetry

Edward Kamens

In the summer of 1600, Hosokawa Yūsai, an aristocratic military man in his mid-sixties, was under siege in Tanabe Castle, near the Japan Sea coast in the countryside north of the capital city. He feared for his life, but he was perhaps even more anxious about the possible destruction of irreplaceable books and literary treatises that he had with him in the castle. Among them were commentaries on the *Kokinshū*, the influential tenth-century anthology of Japanese poetry, and on the *Tale of Genji*, the great eleventh-century narrative, as well as other documents of a centuries-old "secret tradition" of poetic praxis and exegesis called the *Kokin denju*, of which he was the sole living heir. And so he arranged to have some of the most important of his books smuggled out of the castle and delivered to Prince Tomohito, brother of the reigning emperor, Goyōzei, back in the capital. Along with his letter consigning to the prince these treasures and the guardianship of the tradition they embodied, he sent this poem:

> *Inishie mo ima mo kawaranu yo no naka ni*
> *kokoro no tane o nokosu koto no ha*
>
> In this world, unchanging from the past to the present,
> these "leaves of words" preserve the seeds of human feeling.

In proclaiming an identity of past with present (*inishie mo ima mo kawaranu*), Yūsai's poem defied the truth. The battle raging around him was only the most immediate manifestation of forces of epochal change. When the fighting subsided, the "world" he knew would be greatly altered: several hundred years of almost incessant civil warfare would have ended, and a new political order, under the hegemony of one supremely powerful military leader, Tokugawa Ieyasu, would be in place. Against this background of turmoil, Yūsai proclaimed that the traditions of Japanese poetry were an inviolable constant. He turned to the same metaphor that Ki no Tsurayuki (ca. 872–945) had used in his preface to the *Kokinshū*, where he proclaimed that "Japanese poetry has its seed in the human heart (*kokoro*) and finds expression in myriad leaves of words (*koto no ha*)." Yūsai declared once again that the words now inscribed in the treasured books and manuscripts and preserved from the ravages of warfare and other forces of destruction were "seeds of human feeling" (*kokoro no tane*), the best and only means of access to an understanding of poetry, itself the best expression of experience. As long as these texts were not lost, Yūsai suggested, they could yet serve as the source of inspiration and as models for generations of poets still to come. It is only as a poetic act of faith that Yūsai's willful collapsing of past and present seems justifiable. It was a desperate attempt to ignore one kind of reality and affirm another idealized one.

As it turned out, Tanabe Castle was eventually relieved, and Yūsai survived this brush with destruction. But by releasing the *Kokin denju* documents at the height of the crisis, he had insured the survival of that tradition as well. At about the same time, Yūsai also sent a sealed box of additional *Kokin denju* documents to his young friend and literary disciple Karasumaru Mitsuhiro (1579–1638), along with another poem:

> *Moshiogusa kakiatsumetaru ato tomete*
> *mukashi ni kaese Waka no ura nami*
>
> Leave here these traces of sea grasses gathered over time,
> and then return them to the past, oh waves on the shores of "Poetry Bay."

Here, Yūsai used the image of strands of seaweed (*moshiogusa*), gathered for the process of extracting salt from seawater, to represent the many strands of poetic tradition gathered over time and passed down through the *Kokin denju* lineage. His word *kakiatsumetaru* doubles as "raked (as seaweed is raked from the shore) and gathered" and "written (as are texts) and gathered," and thus the meta-

phor is driven toward its literary implication. This is reinforced by Yūsai's use of the toponym *Waka no ura*, evoked for centuries for its suggestion of a place named for Japanese poetry (*waka*) itself; in this case, *ura*, most literally "bay," may also mean "the hidden aspect [of *waka*]," a reference to the secret content of the *Kokin denju*. The presence of such language, hallowed by repeated use in hundreds of earlier poems, is Yūsai's consecration of the passage of the *waka* tradition from his own hands into Mitsuhiro's. It also suggests that the distant past (*mukashi*) is in continuous and direct contact with the present: the waves that roll out of the seas of the past break on a shore where Mitsuhiro stands ready to receive their burden, and then they roll back again into the past. In the event, Mitsuhiro was able to return the box unopened; he would spend a few more years under Yūsai's tutelage before formally receiving the *Kokin denju* transmission from his master.

A respect, even a reverence, for the usages of the literary past was at the core of what was imparted to Mitsuhiro during the years of his intellectual apprenticeship to the much older Yūsai. According to his own record of the relationship, it was in the spring of 1598 that Mitsuhiro, then barely twenty years old, began to pay frequent visits to Yūsai's residence at Yoshida, a district within Kyoto, the capital city; occasionally, Yūsai also called on Mitsuhiro in his own home. Eventually, Mitsuhiro recorded Yūsai's wide-ranging comments on practical aspects of poetic composition, drawn from conversations held at various times between 1598 and 1602—both before and after the Tanabe Castle incident—in an anecdotal treatise he called *Jiteiki*, "a record of words that echo in my ear."[1] Some of their talks took place on evenings after they had attended performances of Nō plays; sometimes, Yūsai himself would take up a drum to accompany an informal reprise (*ranbu*) of a dance highlight of one of the plays they had seen, and on one occasion he also cut up the fish that was to be served for their refreshment.[2] Following these casual entertainments, the conversation inevitably turned to the subject of poetry, with Mitsuhiro posing questions and Yūsai responding extemporaneously. Though natural extensions of the evening's diversions, these conversations touched on the matters that meant most to these two men, and Mitsuhiro eventually decided that they should be written down.

In the *Jiteiki* conversations, the words, practices, and views of one poet of earlier times were cited more frequently, and with more reverence, than any other, and that poet is Fujiwara Teika (1162–1241). This is not surprising, given Teika's stature in the tradition about which Mitsuhiro was seeking special knowledge and guidance through Yūsai. For one thing, Teika was seen as a progenitor of the *Kokin denju* itself, since a number of the commentaries on the *Kokinshū* and other works that were part of the *Kokin denju* corpus were based on Teika's studies.[3] But Teika's name was also closely linked to almost every other text that had come to comprise the central literary canon. He had created authoritative versions of the *Kokinshū* and many other important early works of poetry and prose, including the *Tales of Ise* (*Ise monogatari*) and the *Tale of Genji* (*Genji monogatari*), by gathering and collating manuscripts extant in his own time. The *Shin* ("new") *kokin wakashū* compiled by Teika and others under the direction of the retired emperor Gotoba in the first decade of the thirteenth century had come to be regarded with almost as much reverence as the *Kokinshū* itself. The *Shin kokin wakashū* (or *Shin kokinshū*) was valued particularly as a demonstration of a momentous stage in the evolution of the *waka* tradition, a stage at which its legacy, reaching back to and beyond the *Kokinshū*, was acknowledged anew, while at the same time new realms of intense poetic expression were explored. Many of the poems that came to be thought of as the best examples of *Shin kokinshū* achievement were Teika's own. Also, Teika's widely studied treatises on stylistics (largely collections of model verses, both ancient and contemporary)

---

1. See Karasumaru Mitsuhiro, *Jiteiki*, in Sasaki Nobutsuna, ed., *Nihon kagaku taikei* (Tokyo: Kazama Shobō, 1956), 6: 142–208.
2. *Jiteiki*, Keichō 5.5.4, pp. 189–90. On this occasion, Yūsai played the drum to accompany the dance from the play *Seiōbo* (*The Queen Mother of the West*).
3. The *Kokin denju* lineage actually begins with Teika's grandson, Fujiwara Tameuji, also regarded as the founder of the Nijō school of orthodox poetic practice and criticism. For several generations, the *Kokin denju* was the exclusive property of Nijō school poets. In the fifteenth century, it was a retired warrior, Tō Tsuneyori, who transmitted it to the *renga* (linked verse) master Iio Sōgi; Sōgi bequeathed it to the distinguished courtier and poet Sanjōnishi Sanetaka, from whom it passed to his son Kin'eda, and then to Kin'eda's son Saneki. At his death, Saneki passed the legacy on to Yūsai.
4. *Jiteiki*, Keichō 4. [intercalary] 3.25, p. 175. *Eiga no taigai* (compiled ca. 1221) and *Shūka daitai* (compiled 1222–1226, or as late as 1231) are two of Teika's collections of exemplary verses selected from the imperial anthologies. *Uchūgin* and *Miraiki* were traditionally attributed to Teika but may have been compiled by later Nijō masters; they illustrate styles, rhetorical devices, and techniques to be avoided in *waka* composition.
5. Authorship of the play is usually attributed to Konparu Zenchiku. For a text, see Yokomichi Mario and Omote Akira, eds., *Yōkyokushū 2* (*Nihon koten bungaku taikei* 41), (Tokyo: Iwanami Shoten, 1963), pp. 46–53.

and his own selective anthologies—especially the famous *Hyakunin isshu* (One hundred poems by one hundred poets)—were held in very high esteem. As Yūsai told Mitsuhiro in one of their conversations:

> The "One hundred poems by one hundred poets" should be consulted constantly. Teika selected its contents as a guide for later generations. Then there are his "Essentials of poetic composition" (*Eiga no taigai*) and "Fundamentals of excellent poetry" (*Shūka daitai*). His "Composing in the rain" (*Uchūgin*) and "Records for the future" (*Miraiki*) should be memorized. Through proper study of these poetics, one should be able to distinguish the good from the bad with accuracy.[4]

But what Teika really represented for Yūsai and Mitsuhiro was, in a sense, the *waka* tradition itself and, specifically, a particular feature of that tradition: its constant reuse of its own past.

Of course, by the end of the sixteenth century, Teika's name had come to be virtually synonymous with high culture and with *waka*, its most central and prestigious literary genre. As a sort of culture hero, Teika was apotheosized in many ways, and in various contexts. There was, for example, a play in the repertoire of the Nō theater called "Teika," an extrapolation from a few of his poems and those of his contemporary, the Imperial Princess Shokushi (or Shikishi), conflated with several legends about the two of them—particularly the story that they had shared a great but frustrated passion for one another. Teika is not a character in the play, but his poetic spirit is invoked throughout it, embodied in the words of several of his own poems.[5]

Teika was revered in other settings as well. Even the most fragmentary examples of his rather eccentric calligraphy were highly sought, and his style was widely imitated (Fig. 7; Cat. 1). Renderings of some of his poems by other hands, such as may be seen in a poem slip attributed to Emperor Goyōzei (Fig. 6; Cat. 2), often graced the alcoves of tea rooms where the great masters of *chanoyu*, the tea ceremony, entertained their patrons and instructed their disciples. Thus, the spirit of Teika, embodied in his words, was invoked to impart to the performance of the tea ceremony something of the air of a tradition of intense aesthetic refinement whose history and development were in some sense traceable to him, despite the fact that the tea ceremony itself was unknown in his own day. To seventeenth-century tea masters, a fragment of a text written in Teika's own hand was a fragment of a distant, admired past, but a past in which some continuities with the present could be perceived.

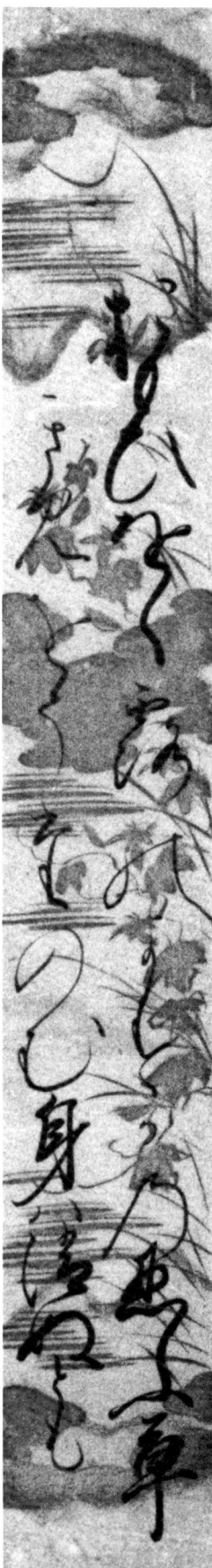

Fig. 6. Attributed to Emperor Goyōzei. *Teika Poem Written on Poem Slip* (Cat. 2).

His controlled, quiet intensity, expressed in the angular strokes of his calligraphy or in the complex layers of meaning and nuance worked into the language of his poems, was something the great tea masters wished to cultivate as an aesthetic principle within the evolving tradition of *chanoyu*.

For Yūsai and Mitsuhiro, Teika was also something of a cult figure. Yūsai cites Teika as the ultimate and unquestioned authority on poetic matters of all kinds. There is also a tendency, as in Yūsai's and Mitsuhiro's poems cited above, to collapse historical time when Teika's position in the *waka* past is assessed:

Mitsuhiro: Did Shōyōin [Sanjōnishi Sanetaka (1455–1537), Yūsai's predecessor in the *Kokin denju* lineage by four generations] ever take issue with anything that Teika said?
Yūsai: No, he did not.
Mitsuhiro: Hitomaro [the great *Man'yōshū* poet, active in the late seventh century], Teika, Sanetaka: in what ways has the style and form [*fūtei*] of the poetry of these three changed and evolved?
Yūsai: It must be said that the times have changed, but really all three are the same. The poems of this threesome are all alike.[6]

The intent of these remarks is to buttress the authority of the *Kokin denju* lineage itself, as well as to support the notion of unwavering continuity and consistency in the *waka* tradition. An absolute sameness is claimed where, of course, close analysis would reveal significant difference as well as correspondence.

Take, for example, the poem by Teika chosen by the retired emperor Gotoba for his imaginary "Poetry Competition for Poets of Different Eras" (*Jidai fudō utaawase*; Fig. 8; Cat. 3)[7]

Hitori nuru yamadori no o no shidario ni
shimo okimayou toko no tsukikage

---

6. *Jiteiki*, Keichō 3.12.25, p. 155.
7. Several decades before Gotoba chose this poem as one of three by Teika to be entered in the imaginary *Jidai fudō utaawase*, it was entered in another great *utaawase*, the *Sengohyakuban utaawase* (Poetry competition in 1500 rounds), carried out on paper rather than in person, and using poems from *hyakushu* (hundred-verse sequences) and other collections submitted by thirty poets. As it happened, Teika was the judge for the section of the *Sengohyakuban utaawase* in which this poem was entered, and out of modesty he proclaimed the poem with which it was paired its superior. Of his own poem he said, "The pheasant's long, drooping tail, the light of the moon on the bed, meandering thoughts on a frosty night: there is something lacking in all these words (*kotoba taranu tokoro ōku*), and it is apparently difficult to ascertain the intended meaning (*kokoro mo wakaregataku haberumeru*)." Nevertheless, the poem was included in the second book of autumn poems in the *Shin kokinshū* no.487.

What looks like frost on the long drooping tail of
   the solitary sleeping pheasant
is actually moonlight falling upon his bed.

Autumnal loneliness, the loneliness of the solitary lover, the difficulty of knowing and understanding what one sees—all this and more is suggested by the poem, descriptive on its surface, complex in the layers of meaning that its language unfolds. On more than one layer, the poem gestures to myriad other poems on pheasants, frost, and moonlight—autumn emblems—but, most particularly, to one poem attributed to Hitomaro in the *Shūishū*, a mid-Heian period anthology:

Ashihiki no yamadori no o no shidario no
naganagashi yo o hitori ka mo nemu

Must I sleep alone through this long, long night,
   long as the drooping tail of the pheasant?

The links between this and Teika's *yamadori* poem are obvious, but it is also obvious that they are very different poems. In Hitomaro's verse, the drooping pheasant's tail (*yamadori no o no shidario*) is invoked as a symbol of length and thus provides access to the word *naganagashi*, "very, very long," which modifies *yo*, "night." The name of the bird is also reached through wordplay of a very special sort, the use of a conventional epithet (a *makurakotoba*), "*ashihiki*," usually applied to the word *yama* ("mountain") but here, by extension, to the *yamadori*, literally "mountain bird." In Teika's poem, the relatively archaic *makurakotoba* is gone, but other elements of Hitomaro's language are still alive, and the pheasant is now present and active in the scene, not just part of a complex word scheme.

Erotic longing is also very active in both poems, though expressed and symbolized in two different ways. It is the overt message of Hitomaro's poem; but that message is conveyed through an elaborated scheme. The "utterer" of Teika's poem feels longing, too, but transfers it to the solitary sleeping bird, which takes on a new role from that which it played in Hitomaro's. It is precisely this mixture of similarity and difference—intriguing, vaguely mysterious, deeply resonant—that makes Teika's poem so remarkable, and also representative of his art. In the long history of *waka* as a cultural institution, Teika stands out as one practitioner who was particularly successful in absorbing and mastering what tradition had bequeathed him and then rendering it anew in accordance with the taste and tenor of his own time. In unique and memorable ways, his poems combined a newly invigorated consciousness of the living literary past with a

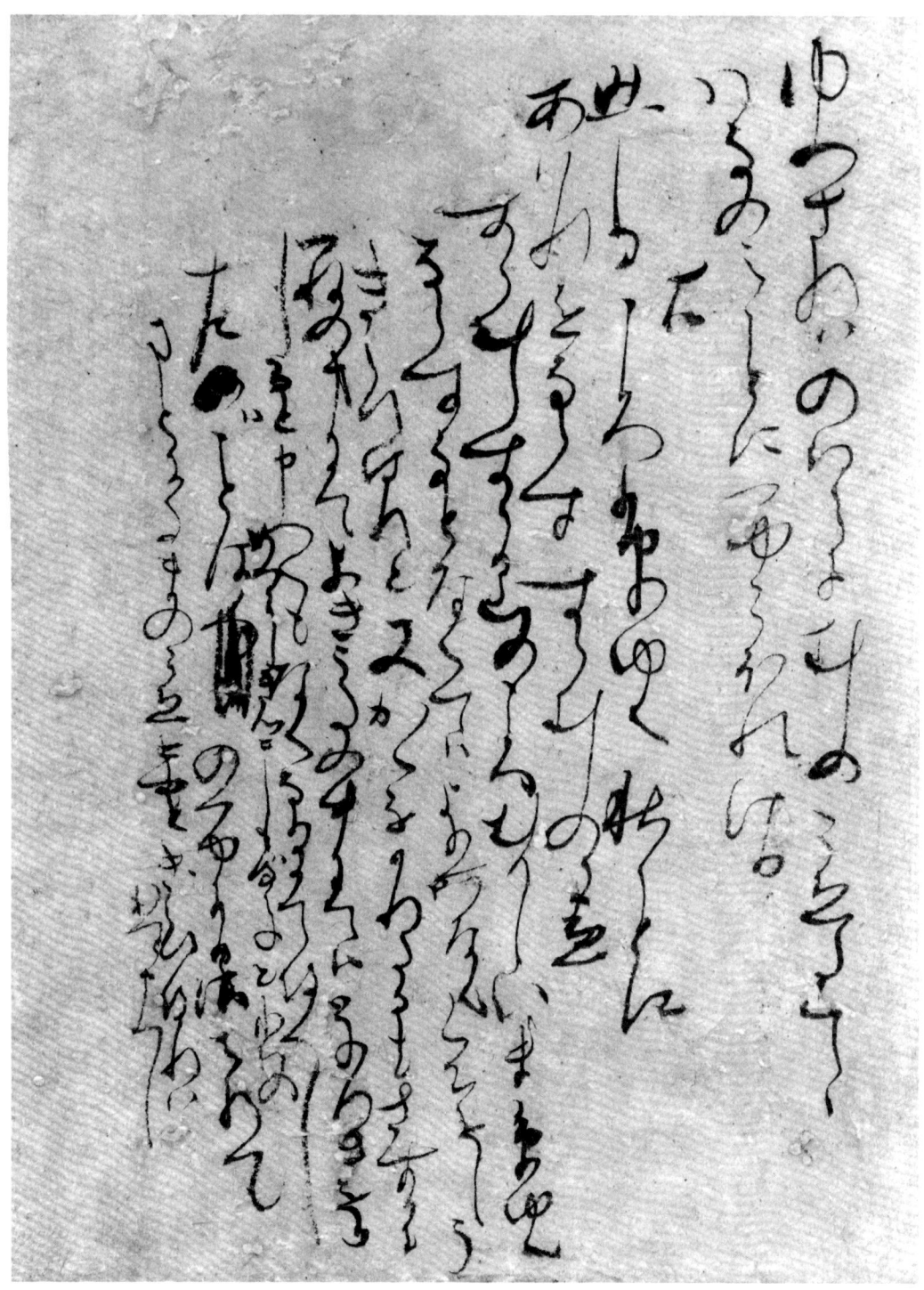

Fig. 7. Attributed to Fujiwara Teika. *Commentary on Poems* (Cat. 1).

heightened intensity and depth of expressiveness that captured the essence of his own "present."

It has become commonplace to describe Japanese cultural history in terms of "continuity and change." Many institutions, values, and forms appear to have remained fixed and to have been communicated from generation to generation in seemingly unbroken lineages; yet in each age they have undergone alterations, retunings to present conditions. Preservation and re-creation of that which is inherited is all-important, but so is the need to be in step with current fashion, to adapt to contemporary circumstances, so the act of re-creation often produces change, generally more subtle than radical. This pattern is very evident in a broad view of the *waka* tradition. Throughout its history (which began well before the seventh and eighth centuries, when songs and poems were first recorded in a script reproducing the sounds of the Japanese language, and carries through to the end of the "premodern" period in the mid-nineteenth century and right up to the present), its major forms remained essentially fixed and its lexicon and rhetorical range varied little. To compose *waka* has always meant to compose within parameters defined by centuries of prior practice, to reproduce familiar features in "new" but not necessarily "original" combinations. Thus, in addition to

"continuity and change," the *waka* tradition is also characterized by an emphasis on "sameness" combined or juxtaposed with "difference," for virtually every individual *waka* calls attention both to its connections with and similarities to an "other"—the past, embodied in a poem or poems of the past—and to its differences from that past and those poems. To this sort of art, Teika was heir, and his profession was the cultivation of it.

In evaluating the poems of others—in judgments at public, "live" poetry competitions (*utaawase*), where the offerings of teams of poets were matched and criticized, or in the judgments recorded in "imaginary" *utaawase* contrived only on paper, or in his treatises—Teika (like his father Shunzei [1114–1204], before him) used a number of key terms of praise, such as *yūgen* ("mystery"), *yōen* ("ethereal beauty"), and *fukasa* ("depth"). In the conversations recorded in *Jiteiki*, however, Yūsai and Mitsuhiro display little interest in these concepts. Rather, they show keen interest in practical considerations and turn their attention to examples of poems that they can use (as Teika used them in his treatises) as guides and models for their own compositions. And they are particularly interested in Teika's own demonstrations of the technique, or mode of composition, which explicitly involves the manipulation of elements of the poetic past—as in the "pheasant" poem discussed above. This technique is known as *honka dori* (sometimes called "allusive variation")[8]—literally, taking something from an older poem and incorporating it into a new one—and it is one of the hallmarks of Teika's poetry and of the poetry of the *Shin kokinshū* age in general. It was through this procedure, among others, that Teika and his contemporaries sought to regain contact with and reinvigorate the poetry of former times and, at the same time, to achieve new effects in something that could be called a style of the "present."

Mitsuhiro frequently asked Yūsai for guidance in the use of *honka*, the poems on which "allusive variation" might be based, as can be seen in these exchanges:

Mitsuhiro: Is it a good idea to treat as the basis for allusive variation (*honka*) a poem that is itself an allusive variation of another?
Yūsai: Yes, it is. One should use poems up to and including those in the one-hundred poem sequence composed for Retired Emperor Horikawa [in 1102]. And even among those, generally, it is the poems of the best poets that should be used as the basis for allusive variation.
Mitsuhiro: Is there such a thing as composing poems that alter the basic meaning of the *honka*?

---

8. See Brower and Miner, *Japanese Court Poetry*, p. 506.
9. *Jiteiki*, Keichō 3.9.11, pp. 150, 152.
10. *Jiteiki*, Keichō 4. [intercalary] 3.27, p. 177.
11. *Jiteiki*, Keichō 6.11.30, p. 197.
12. *Jiteiki*, Keichō 4.3.1, p. 163.
13. The poems are nos. 362 and 363 in the anthology. They, along with no. 361, a poem by Jakuren, are often referred to as "the three great autumn evening poems" of the *Shin kokinshū*.
14. *Jiteiki*, Keichō 3.12.25, p. 157.
15. In its earliest appearances in poems in the *Man'yōshū*, the phrase places sovereigns within landscapes which they survey as rulers thereof. In the poem anthologized as *Shin kokinshū* no. 36 ("*Miwataseba yamamoto kasumu Minasegawa yūbe wa aki to nani omoikemu*"), Retired Emperor Gotoba surveys the landscape from his villa at Minase in the manner of his predecessors, but then distances himself from the standard associations of the poetic tradition: although evenings in autumn are the ideal (*yūbe wa aki*), he finds this spring evening surpassingly beautiful. This poem is commemorated and helps set the scene in the opening verses of *Minase sangin hyakuin*, the great one-hundred-verse *renga* sequence composed by Sōgi and two companions at Minase Shrine, near the site of Gotoba's Minase villa, in 1488.
16. *Harubaru to mono todokōrinaki umizura naru ni nakanaka haru aki no hana momiji no sakari naru yori wa, tada sokowakatonō shigereru kagedomo namamekashiki ni.* . . .
17. *Furu yuki wa kiedomo shibashi tomaranamu hana mo momiji mo eda ni naki koro.*

"Though the falling snow is melting, I wish it would stay, if only briefly
now, when there is neither blossom nor colored leaf upon the branch."

Yūsai: No, there is not. What one does is establish the *honka*, and let it dictate whether one says this or that, as you reinterpret it.⁹

Mitsuhiro: Should poems in the *Shin kokinshū* whose authors are not named be used as *honka*? In the *Shin kokinshū*, the Kyōgoku Middle Counselor [Teika] recommended the use of the poems of poets of the past. But how should poets of the present regard the "poets of the past"?

Yūsai: In general, there are five kinds of situations in which the compilers said "the poet is unknown" (*yomibito shirazu*): when the poet was a person of low status; when the poem was by a Buddha or a *kami*; when the poem was someone disgraced in the eyes of the emperor; or in cases when the poet simply was not known. As for the period in which the poem was written, one can usually tell if it is a poem of the Man'yō era [generally, the seventh and eighth centuries—the era of the poems in the *Man'yōshū*, the earliest collection of Japanese verse], and generally the period in which it was written will be clear. However, it has been said that it is best to use poems whose authors are known with certainty as *honka*. When one is alluding vaguely through the language of the poem to a *honka*, it is said, it is certainly best if the poem alluded to is one of which the author is known.¹⁰

Elsewhere, Yūsai quotes one of Teika's most famous formulas (actually coined by his father, Fujiwara Shunzei, and frequently endorsed and elaborated upon by Teika): "[Yūsai said,] 'Just let the words be old ones and the sentiments new (*kotoba furuki kokoro atarashi*)': this is the most fundamental principle. It is the primary goal. Sankōin [Sanjōnishi San'eki, Sanetaka's grandson and Yūsai's own mentor] was always saying, 'A fine poem is one in which the words are old and yet sound new.'"¹¹ Thus does Yūsai place himself in Teika's direct line of inheritors while endorsing Teika's dictum. The goal, for Mitsuhiro and for all other aspiring poets, is to combine old elements skillfully in new ways, just as all their predecessors had sought to do. The old elements are, of course, the words and phrases of other poems summoned to the surface of the composer's memory as he (or she) sets out to create a "new" poem in response to the emotional and environmental conditions of the present. In such a schema, language and emotion clearly are not one: rather, language is an assortment of tools or components available to the craftsman-poet for his creative task. But what, finally, is the objective? The manipulation of resonant language, or the expression of emotion through that language, or both? Yūsai's position on this is made evident in his explication of a potentially ambiguous passage in one of Teika's major treatises, the *Maigetsushō*: "[Yūsai said] 'In the *Maigetsushō*, where it says, "Is clumsy language really worse than a lack of emotion? [*kokoro no kaketaran yori wa, kotoba no tsutanaki nite koso sōrawame*]," it means that a lack of emotion *is* worse than clumsiness of language.'"¹² The priority of inner, emotional content and impact over surface, structural features may also be part of the basis of Yūsai's rejection of an analytical approach to one of Teika's most famous poems:

> *Miwataseba hana mo momiji mo nakarikeri*
> *ura no tomaya no aki no yūgure*
>
> As I gaze out over the scene, there are neither
>   cherry blossoms nor colored leaves;
> autumn evening at a hut by a bay.

Yūsai's first comment on this poem is erroneous: he says it was composed "in envy of" Saigyō's poem "...*shigi tatsu sawa*... [over the marsh where a snipe is rising]," which immediately precedes it in the first book of autumn poems in the *Shin kokinshū*.¹³ The two poems were in fact composed on two completely unrelated occasions. Yūsai then goes on to say: "It is best to look at this poem without any aid of any kind (*nani no te mo naku mitaru ga yoki nari*). This poem is often cited in discussions of *ranbu* [one of the forms of Nō dance, often performed as a separate entertainment]. All arts are of course a single art (*nani no michi mo michi wa hitotsu nari*). Without any aid whatsoever, it nonetheless encompasses a fascinating scene..."¹⁴ Yūsai calls for a direct response to the poem, unmediated by analysis of its referential gestures. These include the reuse of the opening phrase *miwataseba*, which positions the speaker of the poem as the viewer of a landscape here, as it does in countless other poems.¹⁵ A prose passage in the Akashi chapter of the *Tale of Genji*, describing a seaside scene bereft of blossoms or colored leaves—the most stimulating elements of spring or autumn scenes, and the most potent poetic emblems of those seasons—yet still pleasing to the eye,¹⁶ and an anonymous poem from the *Gosenshū* (compiled in the mid-tenth century as a successor to the *Kokinshū*)¹⁷ also resonate in Teika's poem, but Yūsai says nothing of this. Rather, he says that the poem should be approached and accepted as a whole, just as it presents itself; for, just as it is, it encompasses a great deal, like a *ranbu* dance when performed and observed with proper sensitivity and understanding. Yūsai's analogy involves the suggestiveness of both Teika's poem and the *ranbu* dance form: both provide a means of access to something larger than themselves, yet they encompass that larger entity within their limited frames. It is, therefore, to the totality of the poem that Yūsai directs Mitsuhiro's attention rather than to

Fig. 8. Artist unknown. *Portrait of Fujiwara Teika*, from *Jidai fudō utaawase emaki*, ca. 1300 (Cat. 3).

24 Word in Flower

any of its constituent sources, and Yūsai advises Mitsuhiro to respond to it with his heart rather than with his intellect. Kano Tan'yū's visualization of the poem, a painting in ink and light color on silk in a private collection in Japan (Fig. 11), adheres to that same principle.

Yūsai offers advice of a somewhat more practical nature when they discuss procedures for composing on conventional topics. In Teika's time, sequential compositions prepared by individuals (often in hundred-poem sets called *hyakushu uta*) or by groups of poets (in *utaawase* or other communal settings) often took shape as series of poems addressing or fulfilling expectations and potentials inherent in clusters of sequentially arranged topics: emblems (frequently flowers or birds) of the seasons of the year from spring through winter; the progressive phases of love affairs, from first meeting through union and on to parting and regret; or well-known places (*meisho*) in the various provinces, usually arranged in order of increasing distance from the central capital city. Shunzei, Teika, and their peers praised such poems if they demonstrated a faithfulness to the conventions for treating these topics as decreed by prior usage, but not if the faithfulness was slavish; they also looked for something fresh and vibrant in the treatment. (The "old words, new sentiments" principle was in force here, too.) The poetic essence of the topic, whatever it might be, was something that the poet addressing it had to plumb, and that was best done by becoming acquainted with past poems on that topic before attempting one's own. The appendage of extraneous elements—landscape features not conventionally associated with or emphasized in compositions about a particular famous place, for example—was a delicate, even dangerous matter. Yūsai quotes Teika on this, too:

> "'If I am summoned to an equestrian display and, though I am not officially appointed as one of the demonstrating riders, I suddenly appear from a side entrance (*wakido*) and ride beside those who are so designated—this is just as unsatisfactory as are intrusions into a poem of elements extraneous to the topic. There are all sorts of things that can be added that may be extraneous to the topic, but there are some things which simply will not do as aids (*waki*) standing alongside the topic.' These are golden words," [said Yūsai,] "and one should adhere to them assiduously."[18]

On another occasion, Yūsai seemed to be expressing his own views on the best procedures for composing *meisho* poems, but he was in fact in consonance with Teika's views and practices:

> As for introducing elements other than the customary into poems on famous places: if one goes to that place, and hears and sees things before one's own eyes then and there, then, without consultation of the excellent poems about that place written in the past, one may include whatever one wishes in the poem. This is customary. However, if one is composing a poem with a famous place as its topic, one will not be able to know what is appropriate if one does not consult the excellent poems of the past.[19]

As a model of appropriately inventive *meisho* composition, Yūsai cites a poem by Fujiwara Tsunehira (?–1274; *Shoku kokinshū*, book 4, autumn 1, no. 338; originally composed for an *utaawase* in 1251, on the topic "morning grasses [*chōsōka*]"):

> *Shiratsuyu no Tamakura no no no ominaeshi*
> *tare ni kawaseru kesa no nagori zo*
>
> Oh maidenflowers in dew-covered Tamakura Field:
> with whom have you exchanged the pleasures that linger here this morning?

about which he says, "There was nothing the least bit unsatisfactory about this composition. In addition [to 'dew'], the moon, snow, clouds, and mist are all encountered in every place, so of course they can be introduced into any 'famous place' poem."[20]

To illustrate the same point, he might well have used one of Teika's best-known *honka dori* poems, *Shin kokinshū* no. 671 (originally composed for the winter portion of a series of one hundred poems when Gotoba commissioned *hyakushu* sets from a number of poets in 1200):

> *Koma tomete sode uchiharau kage mo nashi*
> *Sano no watari no yuki no yūgure*
>
> There is no shelter in which to rest my horse or brush the snow from my sleeves
> at Sano Crossing on this snowy night.

Sano Crossing is a ford on a river on the route taken by pilgrims to the Kumano Shrine. Gotoba

---

18. *Jiteiki*, Keichō 4.2.3, p. 158. This particular conversation took place as Mitsuhiro was accompanying Yūsai on his way back to the capital from a diplomatic mission in the province of Tanba. Yūsai's recollection of Teika's illustration of the notion of topical extranea by the image of a superfluous equestrian may have seemed quite appropriate if the two men themselves were traveling on horseback.
19. *Jiteiki*, Keichō 4.3.21, p. 168.
20. Ibid., pp. 168–69. In most texts, the poem reads "*tare to kawaseru*," whereas *Jiteiki* has "*tare ni kawaseru*." The erotic suggestions of the toponym *Tamakura no* ("arm-pillow field") are heightened in combination with *ominaeshi*, which contains "*omina*," "young girl." In editions other than the *Shinpen kokka taikan*, this poem is *Shoku kokin wakashū* no. 340.

himself made the journey many times—his first Kumano pilgrimage was in the eighth month of 1198, shortly after his abdication—and on several occasions Teika was part of his retinue. But Sano Crossing was a "real" place for them, even without "seeing it with their own eyes," because of its earlier appearances in the *waka* tradition, particularly in this *Man'yōshū* poem by Naga no Imiki Okimaro, a contemporary of Hitomaro:

> Kurushiku mo furikuru ame ka
> Miwa ga saki Sano no watari ni ie aranaku ni
>
> How hard the rain is falling!
> But there is no shelter at Sano Crossing on Miwa Cape.[21]

Both poems create the illusion that the poem-speaker is in fact a traveler at Sano, exposed there to the harsh elements. In Teika's poem, this impression is intensifed by the image of snow-covered sleeves; they are the medium through which the traveler comes into physical contact with the environmental forces that envelop him. There are other overt differences between the two poems: Teika omits "Miwa Cape," changes *ie* (house) to *kage* (sheltered place), and—in a move that provides a good basis for Yūsai's advice about the interchangeability of natural elements associated with conventional poetic places—substitutes "snow" for "rain."

Still, the "new" poem's links to the "old" ones are unmistakable, and once again Teika's poem achieves its effect by displaying itself as both "same" and "different." In its praise, the great Nō playwright and theorist Zeami (1363-1443) said: "It is a great poem, and inherently its sound is very pleasing; but one cannot say precisely what it is that is so pleasing about it. . . . It is the same with a fine actor's performance: it produces a feeling that cannot be expressed in words."[22] Yūsai's favorite form of praise, to the effect that a poem can and should be appreciated without mediation (*nani no te mo naku*), reflects a similar approach. In a seventeenth-century visualization of "Sano Crossing" attributed to the school of Tawaraya Sōtatsu (Fig. 9; Cat. 4), the image of the traveler astride his steed is enough to evoke the many associations of the place; the poem is not inscribed in the painting, but its echoes are distinct.

The principle that the potential inherent in a given topic can be realized in more than one way—both through direct experience and through an indirect, intellectual approach based on the study of model works on the same topic—is one that Teika himself espoused. And application of the principle was not limited to the sphere of poetry alone: it also came into play when poetry interacted with painting, another art in which balances between tradition and innovation, sameness and difference were continuously in flux. In 1207, when Gotoba commissioned the construction of a new Buddhist monastery, the Saishō Shitennōin, in Kyoto—as a votive act designed to abet his drive to unseat the Kamakura shogunate—he asked Teika to supervise part of its interior decoration. Teika laid plans for a series of paintings of "famous places" from all over Japan, inscribed with poems, to be mounted on sliding screen doors throughout the building. This pictorial and textual scheme was to give visual form to the objective that underlay the construction of the monastery in the first place: national unification under the imperial house. The project was already well under way when one of the master court painters under Teika's supervision, Sōnai Kaneyasu—whose assignment included the depiction of two especially famous places in Settsu Province, Akashi and Suma (best known through their association with the protagonist's years of exile in the *Tale of Genji*)—came to him with a problem. The weight of tradition, convention decreed by prior treatment of these subjects, was too much for him. "There are so many views about the proper way to treat *meisho*," he complained, "that I am finding it difficult to paint. Akashi and Suma are no great distance from here. If I were to go there and then were to present my plan for painting those scenes, after seeing them with my own eyes, would it cause too great a delay?" Teika replied: "This project does need to be completed as quickly as possible. But we would not want to commit errors, either now or for future viewers. If you paint these scenes after having traveled there yourself, your paintings will surely earn the praise of future generations. I suppose it will not matter, then, if you finish a bit late."[23]

The Saishō Shitennōin paintings did not survive, but one assumes that while some, like Kaneyasu's

---

21. *Man'yōshū* book 3, no. 365.
22. Zeami Motokiyo, *Yūgaku shudō fūken*. See Nishio Minoru, ed., *Nōgakuron shū* (Nihon koten bungaku taikei 41) (Tokyo: Iwanani Shoten, 1961), pp. 444–45.
23. Quoted in Kubota, *Fujiwara Teika*, p. 187.
24. The poem is also included in *Shin chokusenshū* (edited by Teika himself), as no. 143 in the book of summer poems.
25. It was believed that cassia trees grow on the moon.
26. *Jiteiki*, Keichō 4.[intercalary] 3.25; p. 175. In most editions the poem reads "sora no hikari ni ikuyo naruramu."
27. A small section of a handscroll of *Flowers and Birds of the Twelve Months* attributed to Mitsuhiro is reproduced in *Kokka* 201 (1902): 586; the entire work has not been published, and its present whereabouts are unknown.
28. Kubota, ed., *Yakuchū Fujiwara Teika zenkashū*, 1:299.

26 Word in Flower

depictions of Suma and Akashi, were based on direct observation and strove for fidelity to "the real thing," others were designed as evocative re-creations and reinterpretations of traditional treatments of very familiar subjects. Like the poems inscribed with them, these paintings were "new" renderings of something very old, and therein resided their power and appeal.

This was neither the first nor the last time that Teika was so directly involved in projects wherein poetry and painting were conjoined; he and his contemporaries were often called upon to fulfill such commissions for royal patrons. In accordance with traditions that extended back at least to the ninth century—the time of Ki no Tsurayuki—screens (byōbu) were often prepared to commemorate auspicious events at court: annual rituals of kingship, important birthdays of emperors and officials, weddings, and the like. Frequently, the poems and paintings inscribed on the screens were arranged in cyclical sequences—most frequently, the cycle of the seasons, often subdivided into the twelve months of the year with their standard emblems—or in series of meisho representative of the various regions of Japan. Meisho screens, like those at the Saishō Shitennōin, thematically endorsed kingship; seasonal or "twelve-month" (tsukinami) screens, illustrating the course of life cycles in nature, provided fertile ground for the themes of vitality and renewal, and poems composed for them often took the form of expressions of hope for the royal subject's health and longevity. Such is the case, for example, in a poem by Teika on the heartvine, the emblem of the fourth month, prepared for a "twelve-month" screen (tsukinami byōbu) presented on the occasion of the arrival at court of Shunshi, consort of Emperor Gohorikawa, in 1229.[24] Its full meaning becomes clear, as Yūsai explains it, only when the circumstances of its composition are understood:

> Mitsuhiro: What is the meaning of Teika's poem,
> *Hisakata no katsura ni kakuru ahuhigusa*
> *sora no hikari to ikuyo naruramu*
> Oh heartvine draped on the celestial cassia tree, how long will you illuminate the heavens?
>
> Yūsai: The cassia (katsura) is of course associated with the moon.[25] This poem was written on the occasion of a consort's presentation at court, so he used the words "the illumination of the heavens" (sora no hikari) to suggest the "dwelling in the clouds" [i.e., the lofty dwelling, kumoi, of the imperial family]. It was said by way of felicitation.[26]

In other words, Teika personifies the new consort as the heartvine itself, now gracing a celestial space with its beauty just as the moon graces the night sky; he hopes it will continue to do so for "many nights" and "many years" (ikuyo) beyond this initial "day of meeting," the word for which—ahuhi—is embedded in the name "heartvine" (ahuhigusa). The poem is an intricate web of familiar thematic associations appropriate to the specific topic, the heartvine, and the specific event, the imperial wedding; it does what hundreds of earlier congratulatory poems do with commonly shared materials but combines them in a new way to honor the moment and the occasion at hand.

Yūsai took the right approach in explaining this poem to Mitsuhiro: like so many of Teika's poems, it needs to be considered as part of a larger whole, a serial and cyclical compositional scheme conceived for a special and specific function, for the pleasure of important patrons. *Waka* did perform such social and political functions in Teika's time, just as it did in Tsurayuki's and continued to do in Yūsai's and Mitsuhiro's; so continued study of the poetry of the past was never simply an aesthetic pursuit but also was always a practical necessity. Surely both sets of concerns lay behind the surge of interest shown toward certain portions of Teika's oeuvre in the seventeenth century. Mitsuhiro himself may even have been one of the first to revive interest in his *Poems on Flowers and Birds of the Twelve Months*, a cycle of twenty-four *waka* that Teika composed in 1214 at the request of one of Gotoba's sons, Imperial Prince Dōjo Hōshinnō (?–1249), for inscription with screen paintings in the prince's private residence.[27] Again, as in the case of the Saishō Shitennōin screens, the paintings, if ever executed, do not survive; but the poems do, in Teika's own collection of his works, called *Shūigusō*, where they are introduced thus: "I received word from *Go ninnaji no miya* [Dōjo Hōshinnō] that he needed poems on the flowers and birds of the twelve months to be inscribed on paintings, and that if it proved difficult to make a good selection of old poems, I should then compose new ones for him, and so [I wrote these poems]."[28] Apparently, the prince might have been satisfied with a selection of "classic" bird and flower poems by poets of former times, but Teika preferred to create new ones characteristically engaged with their many models in the past. They apparently did meet with the prince's favor, according to an entry in Teika's diary, the *Meigetsuki*, dated Kenpō 2 (1214), second month, thirtieth day:

> At about midday, I went to the royal residence at Ninnaji. Recently, I had been commanded to compose a set of poems. Having completed their composition in the manner specified, I took them and

presented them. As the Prince was bathing, he did not grant me an audience, but he repeatedly sent word out to me through intermediaries. Thus it was communicated to me that he had received with great pleasure the humble poems I had offered. I thereupon withdrew.[29]

What was it that so pleased Dōjo Hōshinnō? Surely, the poems presented rich material for illustration. They could be read, and visualized, as skilled realizations of the potential that had accrued to these topics through prior usage. For centuries—at least as far back as the *Man'yōshū*—these flowers and birds had been associated with specific seasons and months of the year, but they were also invariably treated as symbols: for example, the *ominaeshi*, an autumn bloom, represented young female charm (especially because of its name, which suggests "maidenflower"), and mandarin ducks (*mizutori* or *oshi*), said to mate for life, stood for constancy. In their manipulations of these and other conventions for the treatment of flowers and birds as set topics, Teika's poems incorporated many gestures to the traditions of the past, including the tradition of felicitous screen painting-and-poem presentation itself. Many of the poems were, of course, *honka dori* poems, and thus, through their allusive operations, they gave deeper resonance to the whole, an entity conceived for practical and enjoyable use in the present but modeled on the customs of the past.

When seventeenth-century painters took up Teika's *Flowers and Birds of the Twelve Months* as their subject, they must have done so with a strong sense of the text's grounding in the past and its potential for resonating in the present. For one version, the pair of screens by Yamamoto Soken in the Yale University Art Gallery (Fig. 16; Cat. 6) twelve distinguished courtiers, all skilled calligraphers, collectively reproduced the poems. Perhaps they were also the commissioners of Soken's painting: they may have viewed the finished product as an attractive and inspiring model for other creative projects, or perhaps they were simply interested in reenacting a creative moment recalled from a time almost five hundred years before their own. As they looked at Soken's paintings and read the poems—so full of allusions to the known and to the imaginable past—the links between other times and theirs may have seemed as direct and firm as Yūsai, Mitsuhiro, and other poets would have liked them to be. The facts may have been otherwise, but the pleasant illusion may have been irresistible.

For seventeenth-century poets, painters, and calligraphers, Teika and his works were by no means the only models for the invigorating reuse of the past. Still, his poems, and other works closely associated with him, including the *Shin kokinshū* as a whole as well as *The Tales of Ise* (see "Images of the *Tales of Ise*"), were among their most favored texts. In them, as Teika had done in his own time, they found boundless room for new expression, but expression inextricably linked through its subject matter to the past—to Teika's time, and to times before and after him. These artists' use of the past, like his, continued the process of identifying the traditions and achievements of former periods as texts inviting constant and repeated revisitation and reexploration. This was the nature of their classicism: they had only to reach out, and there, available to them, were these great model texts, inviting new encounters and presenting opportunities for new appropriations continuously through time. In Teika's deserted bay viewed at the end of an autumn day there may have been no blossoms or colored leaves, but every ripple breaking on the shore bore riches from the distant, living past and deposited them again and again in the present.

Fujiwara Teika: Poems on the Flowers and Birds of the Twelve Months

THE FIRST MONTH

Willow (*yanagi*)

Uchinabiki haru kuru kaze no iro nareya
hi o hete somuru aoyagi no ito

Is this color that of the wafting breeze that brings the spring?
With each passing day the waving strands of willow are dyed a deeper green.

Warbler (*uguisu*)

Haru kite wa iku yo mo suginu
asato ideni uguisu kiiru mado no muratake

Spring has only been here for a few nights,
but when I step outside my door in the morning I find the warbler in the bamboo by my window.

---

29. Imagawa, ed., *Kundoku Meigetsuki*, 4:12.

Fig. 9. School of Tawaraya Sōtatsu. *Sano Crossing* (Cat. 4).

Re-Presenting Teika's Flowers and Birds

Kendall Brown

Old and new at the same time, *Teika's Poems on Flowers and Birds of the Twelve Months* may be called a newly classicized classic. Paintings of the theme provide a model of how individual artists were able simultaneously to classicize and modernize *Teika's Poems*. On the one hand, both the literary source and the dominant representational modes of these paintings are linked to courtly culture. Seventeenth- and early-eighteenth-century audiences saw Teika as the foremost classical litterateur and seasonal poems of flowers and birds as a central theme of the Japanese poetic tradition. They recognized the brightly colored *yamato-e* manner of depiction as the traditional style of the imperial court. On the other hand, as a painting theme, *Teika's Poems on Flowers and Birds* was positively new: there is no evidence that it was illustrated before the seventeenth century. Thus, *Teika's Poems* carried neither the authority nor the burden of other classical literary works such as the *Tales of Ise* and the *Tale of Genji*. The theme it presented was flexible and thus relatively free to evolve a variety of possible meanings and artistic interpretations.

Of the roughly twenty known paintings on *Teika's Poems*, nearly three-quarters were produced between 1650 and 1710. And although the theme was depicted by artists representing a variety of schools, almost all of these artists worked in the Kyoto region—the heartland of traditional Japanese culture. Despite their similar locus in time and place, these artists interpreted *Teika's Poems on Flowers and Birds* in different ways. Their visualizations of the written text express varying attitudes toward the classical past. In particular, four distinct interpretative types stand out.

Tosa Mitsuoki, leader of the Tosa school in the mid-seventeenth century, and Kano Tan'yū, head of the Kano school, both created independent and influential paintings of the theme. In the next generation, Yamamoto Soken, a Kano student influenced by the Tosa style, fused elements of both traditions into a new vision of *Teika's Poems*. Finally, Soken's student Ogata Kenzan reexplored the fundamental issue of text and image to reinterpret the classical subject in a new artistic and social context. In diverse ways, all of these artists self-consciously borrowed motifs, styles, and even meanings from the past and then manipulated those elements to create new visions from old reflections.

It is significant that Teika's poetry was turned to as the subject of paintings done in the seventeenth and early eighteenth centuries. For the elite of this period—the court and military aristocracy, the wealthy but disenfranchised merchants, and the artists who helped shape their taste—Teika was a monumental figure, a virtual paradigm for the creation of new modes of expression from old ones. In aesthetic terms, Teika's technique of *honka dori*, "allusive variation" (see above, p. 22) was a model for the re-creation of the present from the past. The late-seventeenth- and early-eighteenth-century paintings of *Teika's Poems on Flowers and Birds* frequently work in the same way as the poems do. The subjects are conventional but the effects are undeniably new. Thus, these paintings express a continuity with the classical past that yet legitimizes the values of the present. In essence, classical elements act as the fulcrum by which the past is brought to bear upon the present, sanctifying it with the weight of old aristocratic culture but employed lightly enough, and changed significantly enough, to create something tangibly modern.

The relation of painted image to poetic text, central to understanding these works, is remarkable in the very way the poems were created: the fact that they were originally commissioned for inscription on screens (see above, pp. 27–28) suggests that Teika may have composed them to relate specifically to

Fig. 10. Yamamoto Soken. *Teika's Poems on Flowers and Birds of the Twelve Months*, detail of the second month (Cat. 6).

Fig. 11. Kano Tan'yū (1602–1674). *Portrait of Fujiwara Teika*. Hanging scroll, ink and light color on silk, 28.0 x 39.6 cm. Sōji-ji, Tokyo. Published in Takeda, *Kano Tan'yū*, col. pl. 36, p. 134. Inspired by Teika's famous poem, *Shin kokinshū*, no. 363.

> *Miwataseba hana mo momiji mo kakarikeri*
> *ura no tomaya no aki no yūgure*
>
> "As I gaze out over the scene, there are neither cherry blossoms nor colored leaves;
> autumn evening at a hut by a bay"

Fig. 12. Tosa Mitsuoki (1654–1691). *Teika's Poems on Flowers and Birds*. Detail of sixth month. Handscroll, ink and color on silk, Tokyo National Museum. Entire scroll published in Takeno, *Museum* 414, pp. 8–9; and in Nishimoto, *Kokka* 1043, pp. 24–25; color details in Kobayashi and Murashige, *Shōsha sōshokubi*, col. pls. 59–60.

visual images.[1] The seventeenth-century production of paintings of these poems seems to stem from a renewed interest in Teika's poetry. More than one scholar has suggested that aristocrats, as well as upper-class samurai and merchants, used *Teika's Poems on Flowers and Birds*, and paintings of them, as evidence of their erudition.[2] Indeed, *Teika's Poems* generally are written right on the surface of the paintings or are affixed to the screens depicting them. The poems are not distant progenitors of, but, in varying ways, active participants in the paintings.

---

1. Research by Adachi Keiko has determined that the earliest recorded pure flower-and-bird paintings are those for which Teika wrote his poems. *Kokka* 1083 (1985): 17.
2. Nishimoto, "Ogata Kōrin hitsu jūnikagetsu utai-e byōbu ni tsuite," *Kokka* 1006 (1977): 10, and Tanomura, *Kokka* 803 (1959): 43–44.
3. The earliest recorded example of the theme is a handscroll with calligraphy and rough sketches by the courtier Karasumaru Mitsuhiro (1579–1638). A small section of the handscroll is reproduced by Taka Seiichi in "Calligraphy in Connection with Painting and Decorative Arts," *Kokka* 201 (1902): 586, but the entire work has not been published and its current location is unknown.

12

The earliest known painting of *Teika's Poems* is a pair of handscrolls by Tosa Mitsuoki (1617–1691) in the Tokyo National Museum, dated between 1651 and 1681.[3] These handscrolls alternate sections of text—the two poems for each month—with illustrations of the poems. The word *illustration* is appropriate here because Mitsuoki not only meticulously represented the explicit narrative elements of the poems but added figures and structures merely implied in the poems or loosely associated with Teika's images. Although Teika specifically mentions human beings only in his poems for the second month and describes human dwellings only in his poems for the fifth and eighth, Mitsuoki featured human figures and houses in his pictures for six of the months. For example, in the bird poem of the sixth month, Teika's poem on cormorant fishing prompted Mitsuoki to paint a nocturnal scene, with two men in a boat fishing with cormorants by the light of a flare (Fig. 12). Behind the fishermen is a cave with craggy pines and fishing weirs among reeds. Scarcely visible in the lower right-hand corner of the scene appears the flower taken from the flower poem of the sixth month—the pink (*tokonatsu*). Perhaps because this flower poem implies no obvious human action, Mitsuoki virtually ignored it. Mitsuoki's picture scrolls display a narrative sensibility, in that his superfidelity to the visual surface of some of Teika's poems resulted in his creating a series of genre scenes that suggest the telling of a story.

That Mitsuoki's paintings borrow the format of illustrated narrative scrolls, sections of text followed by illustrations, further encourages a narrative reading of the poems and pictures. Like his Tosa school predecessors, he specialized in illustrating classical narratives. His treatment of *Teika's Poems on Flowers and Birds* appears to be a conscious effort to fit this new subject—classical, but lacking an extant visual history—into the well-established mode of depicting classical literary themes. Mitsuoki's conservative interpretation successfully imbues *Teika's Poems* with a classical aura and a sense of history, both in time and in visual style. Yet, because Teika's text is poetry rather than narrative prose, there is an inherent disjunction between text and image in these paintings. In the pictures for some months, the narrative-like description of one poem tends to obscure the other; while, on a broader level, the scrolls alternate between scenes that are essentially genre figure paintings and others that are pure

Fig. 13. Kano Tan'yū (1602–1674). *Teika's Poems on Flowers and Birds*. Detail of fifth and sixth months. Pair of six-panel screens, ink and color on silk. University of Michigan Museum of Art. Reproduction of entire screens in Takeno, *Museum* 414, pp. 11–12.

flower and bird paintings. In short, Teika's poetic text is visualized as a set of separate units rather than as an integral whole.

Mitsuoki's interpretation of *Teika's Poems on Flowers and Birds* as a prose text to be described in visual terms was adapted by later Tosa artists. Mitsunari (1646–1710), for instance, transferred his father Mitsuoki's basic approach to the folding-screen format. His pair of six-panel screens in the Tiger Collection (Fig. 15), echoes Mitsuoki's creation of a narrative context for the flower and bird pictures. Unlike the handscroll format, in which text and painting are viewed sequentially, Mitsunari painted a continuous landscape along a consistent ground plane in the lower portion of the screens and filled the upper register with twenty-four square poetry papers, or *shikishi*, inscribed with Teika's poems. In this way, Mitsunari's screens recall the structure of Heian period poem-screens the format of screens for which Teika's poems originally were composed. This recollection of the poem-screen tradition ties Mitsunari's paintings to a format associated both with classical *yamato-e* and, unlike Mitsuoki's handscrolls, with a format that is well suited to the simultaneous presentation of poems and pictures. Because of the accordion-fold configuration of Japanese screens, in which each panel occupies a plane at a right angle to its adjoining panels, there is an independent vertical orientation for each scene. Mitsunari accentuated this separation of scenes by confining his often unnaturally large flowers and trees to single panels and placing two *shikishi* in each panel. The screens thus combine the horizontal alignment of a handscroll and the vertical arrangement of a hanging scroll.

By establishing a consistent space in the screens, Mitsunari surpassed Mitsuoki in grounding his

---

4. In *Nanporoku*, the influential tea treatise of ca. 1593, tea master Takeno Jōō (1502–1555) is quoted as saying that Teika's "*Miwataseba*..." poem is the perfect embodiment of *wabi* tea. See H. Paul Varley, "The Culture of Tea," in George Elison and Bardwell Smith, eds., *Warlords, Artists, and Commoners* (Honolulu: University of Hawaii Press, 1981), p. 327, and Dennis Hirota, "Memoranda on the Words of Rikyū: Namporoku, Book I," *Chanoyu Quarterly* 25 (1980):31–48.

5. Tanomura, *Kokka* 787 (1957): 311–20.

motifs, and by extension the entire theme, in a rich classical atmosphere. The poems are set in a single time and place—the paradisiacal Yamato of the courtly epoch, where courtiers live among singing birds and blossoming flowers. Mitsunari, like Mitsuoki before him, created a storybook classicism. One can well imagine the pleasurable sense of escape felt by the late-seventeenth-century viewer as he looked into these screens. While Mitsunari's and Mitsuoki's inclusion of courtly figures gazing at the flowers and birds of the poems may be interpreted as an invitation to the viewer to share their feelings, the presence of the figures may also serve to distance him from the poems. In effect, the viewer becomes a third party: obliged to watch the experiences of someone else, he is cut off from the poems and cannot participate in them directly. For Tosa artists, Teika's *Poems on Flowers and Birds* seem to have functioned primarily as symbols of a bygone age and culture.

Kano Tan'yū (1602–1674) interpreted Teika's *Poems on Flowers and Birds* very differently from his Tosa school contemporaries. Whereas the Tosa painters' versions are descriptive, Tan'yū's approach is lyrical. He responded to the depth (*fukasa*) of the poems and, in doing so, stressed their status as poems by Teika. Tan'yū is best known as an official painter to the Tokugawa shoguns and as the creator of many monumental wall paintings. His depiction of *Teika's Poems*, however, is related to a lesser-known side of his career. An intimate of Kyoto literary salons and tea circles, he was well acquainted with tea aesthetics. In particular, the influential "refined rusticity" or *kirei sabi* aesthetic of the tea master Kobori Enshū (1579–1647), in which the emphasis on elegant surfaces was fused with underlying poetic depth, seems to have influenced Tan'yū's sensitive visualization of *Teika's Poems*. Tan'yū also was familiar with the Teika cult fostered by Enshū and prominent in the salon of Emperor Gomizunoo (1596–1680). Tan'yū's imaginary portrait of Teika (Fig. 11), inscribed with Teika's "*Miwataseba*..." poem, attests to both the artist's interest in Teika and his expressive treatment of Teika's poetry.[4]

Tan'yū's broadly influential approach to *Teika's Poems on Flowers and Birds* is exemplified by a pair of six-panel screens in the University Art Museum, University of Michigan. Each panel includes the flower and bird for one month independently from the others, perhaps indicating the screen's origin as a set of hanging scrolls. The painting for the sixth month (Fig. 13) demonstrates the originality of Tan'yū's conception. The painted images stand alone: Teika's poems are neither written directly on the painting nor on *shikishi* attached to the screen (although original *shikishi* may have been lost). The flower and bird motifs, enlarged to fill almost the entire picture surface, provide the dominant focus. These large-scale motifs generally refer more strongly to the Kano school flower-and-bird tradition than they do to the small-scale Tosa narrative orientation. There is a marked reduction of architectural elements (of the twelve scenes, only that of the first month includes a human dwelling) and a total absence of human figures. For instance, in the sixth-month picture, Tan'yū painted only the stern of a fishing boat supporting the flare mentioned in the bird poem. In no way do Tan'yū's paintings narrate or imply an imagined action within the poems. Rather, one empathetically senses the poems' mood and spirit.

Tan'yū's style is a large part of his message. His prevalent use of ink wash and loose, fluid brushwork—the very antithesis of the minute detailing and vivid palette of the Tosa style—lends his pictures a quality of misty atmosphere and mysterious depth. He suggested the depth of Teika's poetry through simplification of his own pictorial vocabulary, recalling the brief form of *waka*, combined with an expressive handling of the brush akin to Japanese poetic syntax. In short, Tan'yū translated Teika's form of verbal expression into a visual style.

For Tan'yū, painting a classical theme was a matter of capturing an aesthetic mood. However, other artists borrowed aspects of his style—specifically his compositions and motifs—to create quite different effects. One example can be clearly seen in two sets of folding screens by Yamamoto Soken (fl.1683–1706)—one set in the Yale University Art Gallery (Cat. 6), the other in the Asian Art Museum of San Francisco (Fig. 14). Soken learned the Kano style from his father, Sotei, a leading pupil of Tan'yū, and may have studied with Tan'yū himself.[5] He was a skilled practitioner of the late-seventeenth-century "academic style"—a mix of the elegantly detailed Tosa manner with the bolder forms of traditional Kano painting as synthesized by Tan'yū.

Soken's two pairs of screens are similar in composition; only the pictures for the fifth and seventh months present substantially altered arrangements of the flower-and-bird motifs. They differ, however, in the artist's treatment of the painting surface. While the San Francisco paintings feature a liberal use of light ink wash to break up the surface and create a sense of hazy atmosphere in the manner of Tan'yū's paintings, the Yale screens add a sprinkling of cut silver leaf (now oxidized to black) that creates a visual pull to the surface and adds a distinctly decorative quality.

The variance in surface is echoed in the handling of the text. Both works include Teika's poems written gracefully in staggered vertical registers called "scattered writing," or *chirashigaki*. In the San Francisco screens, the poems and paintings share the same sheet of silk, while the Yale screens feature the poems written on paired *shikishi* decorated with flower-and-bird designs in gold paint. The names and titles of the twelve calligraphers, all high-ranking courtiers, are inscribed in cartouches appended to the right of each pair of *shikishi* (see Cat. 6). The presence of the *shikishi* indicates the courtly context for which the Yale screens likely were intended. Although the calligraphers of the San Francisco scrolls are unknown, the calligraphy, in keeping with Soken's less sumptuous treatment of the surface, exhibits traits often associated with the ink-painting tradition of Zen priests. For example, the flower poem of the ninth month and both poems for the eleventh month are written in reverse order, from left to right—a technique found in the inscriptions of Zen priests. The variant approaches to the painting surface indicate two subtle yet distinct aesthetic stances, and the different treatment of the calligraphed text further suggests that Soken may have been aiming these paintings at slightly different audiences.[6]

In both pairs of screens, written text and visual image work together to convey meaning, with verbal images buttressing visual ones and vice versa. By presenting flower-and-bird "portraits" below and the related poems above, Soken mimicked the compositional structure found in traditional "poet portraits," or *kasen-e*. Like the imaginary portraits of famous poets, Soken's flowers and birds are idealized visions. He lavished attention on naturalistic details, carefully rendering every leaf of the flowers and each feather of the birds. Yet, the combination of a consistent interest in curvilinear forms—flowing streams, bending grasses, the sinuous necks of birds—together with the soft clarity of the flower-and-bird motifs, creates a lyrical effect. This idealization empowers Soken's flowers and birds to represent the specific motifs of Teika's poems and, like the images in the poems, to evoke the broader associations of these same flowers and birds in the corpus of classical literature. Yet, Soken's standard flower-and-bird motifs from the Kano and, occasionally, the Tosa modes similarly carry specific symbolic meanings within the artistic tradition—meanings often different from those found in literature. Soken's ability to elicit reverberations from both the literary and artistic traditions gives his paintings meaning below their beautiful surface and provides an original reinterpretation of *Teika's Poems*.

Soken's imitation of *kasen-e* is more than an idle conceit meant to link his paintings structurally to a classical format of poetry-painting. The implication that the flower-and-bird subjects express the themes of love and longing found in *Teika's Poems* lies at the very heart of the paintings. The idea of using natural motifs as symbols of human emotions is basic to *waka*, and associating flowers and birds with aspects of human character was a standard practice in Chinese and Japanese ink painting. Although one is accustomed to looking beneath the surface of Japanese poetry and painting themes derived from China, this is rarely done when analyzing Edo period decorative flower-and-bird painting. However, to recognize the implications of these motifs is to understand the paintings.

Most of the bird-and-flower motifs in *Teika's Poems* have long-held metaphoric associations. The motifs in Soken's paintings, too, must be read for their symbolic value and, more specifically, as a linked series that forms a narrative. The natural year is marked by twelve monthly units with a nuanced linear progression from one to the next. The annual sequence of months further implies the clustering of monthly groups into four seasons that move cyclically from creation in spring, to fruition in summer, to withering in autumn, and, finally, to death and rebirth in the winter. The progression and association inherent in the twelve months and four seasons provides a natural model for the arrangement of other poetic themes—namely, the progress of love. In *Teika's Poems*, flowers and birds, as symbols of each phase of the natural cycle, are invested with the emotions of human lovers. Although the romantic, even erotic, subtext is only one layer of meaning, it seems to have held the strongest appeal for Soken and his patrons. By highlighting and reinterpreting many of Teika's classical flower-and-bird symbols, Soken visually reread Teika's text, transforming the classical and making it new.

---

6. Another example of a poem inscribed from left to right on a painting of a classical literary subject is Tawaraya Sōtatsu's *Tales of Ise*, Nunobiki Falls (Cat. 29), although in this case the inverted order of text is a compositional ploy, to focus attention on the waterfall.

Fig. 14. Yamamoto Soken (fl. 1683–d. 1706). *Teika's Poems on Flowers and Birds*. Detail of fifth and sixth months. Pair of six-panel screens, ink and color on silk, each screen 312.2 x 113.0 cm. Asian Art Museum, San Francisco. Published in Kobayashi and Murashige, *Shōsha sōshokubi*, appendix (pp. 176–77).

Fig. 15. Tosa Mitsunari. *Teika's Poems on Flowers and Birds of the Twelve Months*, ca. 1688–1710 (Cat. 5).

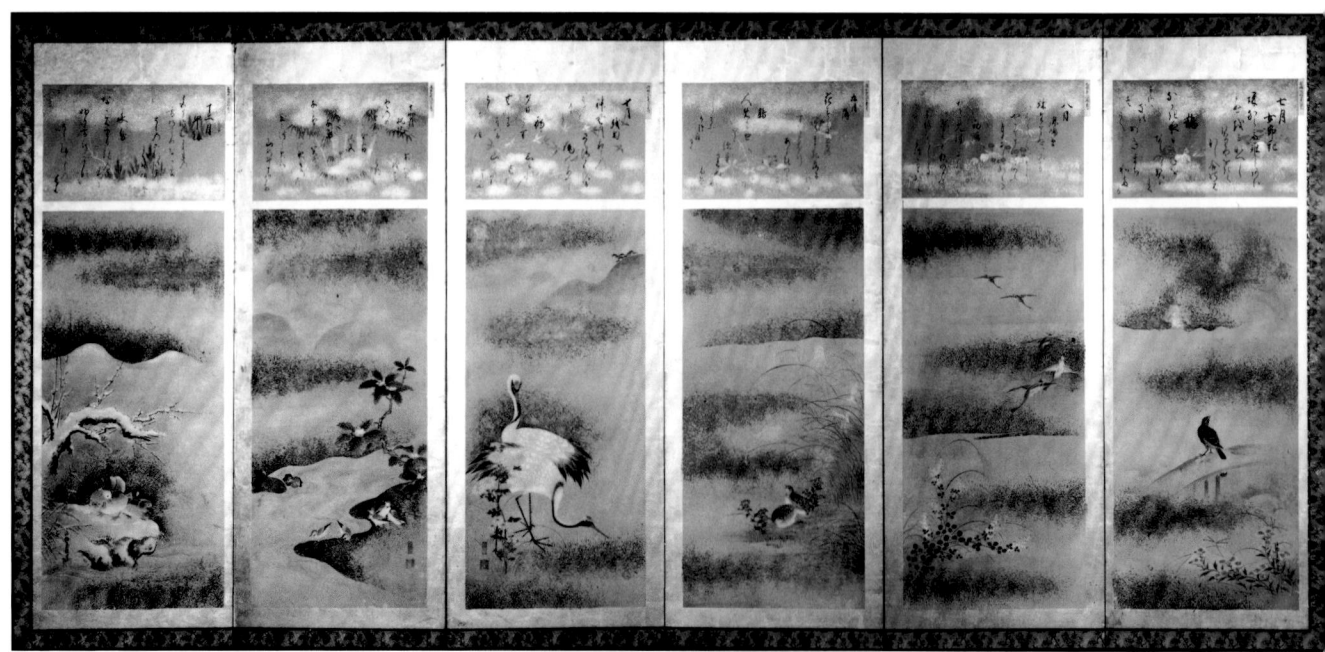

Fig. 16. Yamamoto Soken. *Teika's Poems on Flowers and Birds of the Twelve Months*, ca. 1690–1692 (Cat. 6).

Fig. 17. Tosa Mitsunari. *Teika's Poems on Flowers and Birds of the Twelve Months*, detail of the fifth and sixth months (Cat. 5).

Fig. 18. Yamamoto Soken. *Teika's Poems on Flowers and Birds of the Twelve Months*, detail of the fifth and sixth months (Cat. 6).

The poems and pictures for the first three months, the spring group, begin the narrative with the blossoming of new love. The first month announces the coming of spring, visible in the deepening green of the willow catkins and heralded by the song of the warbler. The mood of expectation is picked up in the second month, when the search for love begins. Teika's flower poem suggests courtiers on a pleasure expedition catching the scent of cherry blossoms, along with willows, a standard symbol for beautiful women.[7] Although the bird poem for the second month combines images of hunters searching for prey and a pheasant calling for its mate, Soken's pictorial conflation of bird-and-flower motifs suggests that it is the pheasant who has caught the scent and is pursuing the flowering cherry, and thus he imposes a new reading on Teika's poem. In the third month, Teika's poem on wisteria and its *honka* share a reflective attitude, while the bird poem and its *honka* evoke the sensuality of love, describing a skylark at ease in a bed of violets—another floral symbol for women. Following the erotic imagery of the poem, Soken shows two skylarks among clumps of violets. The bird now clearly symbolizes the male lover, while the flower is his paramour.

The fourth month signals a change in season and in mood. The bird of the fourth month, the cuckoo, is associated both with the third-month flower, wisteria, and the fifth-month flower, orange, as well as its companion here, deutzia. Soken, following Tan'yū's compositional models, shows a cuckoo flying among the flowers, thereby linking the three plants, moving the action from spring to summer, and metaphorically progressing from an old lover to a new one. Soken's visualization of the fifth month, however, implies sexual intrigue, as a male lover makes a nocturnal visit to the door of the beloved. In Teika's flower poem, the orange awaits the cuckoo that will "lodge among its branches." The implication is that even before the current affair can be consummated, the lover is recalling the past and wondering how it will be remembered in the future. Yet the water rail, a symbol of the aggressively courting male, suggests an interloper. In Teika's bird poem, the water rail tapping at a door recalls section 75 of the *Diary of Murasaki Shikibu*, where the powerful courtier Michinaga appears one night at the author's door, raps, but gaining no entrance, writes a poem comparing his action to the tapping of the water rail.[8] In the San Francisco painting for the fifth month (Fig. 4), Soken, breaking with Tan'yū's motifs, adds a house. He does not merely conform to the imagery of "eaves" in both of Teika's fifth-month poems, as does Mitsunari, but, by showing the water rail strutting toward the door, Soken highlights the implication of sexual adventure.

In the sixth-month poems, summer achieves its sultry peak, and in the pictures the sexual aspect of love reaches its climax. Soken's cormorant, its long, snaky neck plunging into the water, is an image of male sexuality and the beautiful, passive pink—*tokonatsu*, literally, "summer bed" in Japanese—is a traditional symbol for sexually available young women. The erotic thrust of Soken's composition is best seen in comparison with the treatments of Mitsuoki (Fig. 12) and Mitsunari (Fig. 15) of the same scene. Whereas the Tosa artists virtually ignored the flowers to concentrate on the fishermen, Soken's conflation of the fishing boat, cruising cormorant, and summer bed of pinks growing unnaturally along the river's edge, forms a potent visual metaphor of "fishing" for women.[9] None of this is implied in Teika's poems. Soken, it seems, based his visual interpretation on other associations of the flower and bird as they fit into his overtly romantic narrative.

The seventh month shifts the season and mood from the hope and heat of summer to the melancholy of autumn. The nocturnal meeting continues, but now with an undertone of parting. Soken juxtaposes the "maidenflower," another symbol of female sexuality and a sign of autumn, with the magpie, a bird associated with Tanabata, the seventh-month festival of lovers. Teika's bird poem echoes a long line of poems that mention a bridge of magpies' wings, and it is this image that Soken literally represents in the San Francisco screens, while his single magpie atop a bridge in the Yale screens follows iconography established by Mitsuoki and Tan'yū. The idea of parting changes to overt sadness in the eighth month—bush clover and wild geese symbolizing autumn, loneliness, and the impermanence of love. Autumnal melancholy deepens in the ninth month, where quail and deep autumn grasses are emblems of desolation and abandonment. In Teika's poems the quail seems to be a male lamenting his lost love, withered like autumn grasses, and the

---

7. The symbolism was originally Chinese, from a poem by the Tang poet Li Bo. In the late seventeenth century, *karyū*, or "cherry-willow," was a nickname for "geisha," and the pleasure quarters of cities were planted with the two trees.
8. See Bowring, *Murasaki Shikibu, Her Diary and Poetic Memoirs*, p. 145.
9. The term "fishing for women," *tsuri onna*, is the title of a Kyōgen farce.

abandoned miscanthus is soaked with tearlike dew. Soken, however, introduces a note of promise that deviates from the imagery of longing in the poems by depicting a pair of quails, a motif associated with conjugal fidelity in both the Chinese and Japanese painting traditions.

The tenth month changes the season to winter and the poems develop more profoundly the theme of loneliness. In Teika's poems the chrysanthemum is just a memory of autumn, while cranes huddle in a gloomy evening shower. Soken's paintings, however, display a pair of elegant cranes standing next to a stalk of chrysanthemums. Because both the flower and the bird represent long life, one feels that, despite the gloomy season, love remains. Again, Soken turned Teika's melancholy flower and bird into auspicious symbols of longevity, fidelity, and renewal, suggesting a happy ending. The eleventh-month paintings advance this felicitous mood despite the bleak environment of the poems. Soken focuses on the evergreen loquats, symbols of strength and endurance, and the plovers, preeminent Japanese symbols of longevity. The twelfth month completes the year, suggesting the renewal of spring and of love. Teika's poem on the plum is optimistic, as expressed in Soken's depiction of pink flowers blossoming despite the snow. Teika's bird poem, however, is distinctly sad, evoking the figure of a lone mandarin duck covered with snow. In Japanese poetry, the duck, "bird of regret," symbolizes steadfastness and loneliness, remaining alone after the death of its mate. In the painting tradition, however, mandarin ducks are usually depicted in pairs, representing marital fidelity. Soken's pair of ducks huddle together, an image of constancy and endurance under adverse circumstances. He thus conveys the optimistic message that, despite hardship, love can survive.

Understood in another way, the ideas of endurance, longevity, and renascence may also fit attitudes toward court culture in the late seventeenth century. The calligraphers of the poems on the Yale screens, if correctly identified by the cartouches, were all high-ranking courtiers (see Cat. 6). It is tempting to speculate that Soken intended his work to be read at one level as an explicit statement about the vitality of court culture in the aesthetic context of Kyoto society. By focusing on a deep structure of meaning in Teika's text, Soken not only invited his audience to participate in the classical poetic tradition but also brought that tradition into the present through visual reinterpretation.

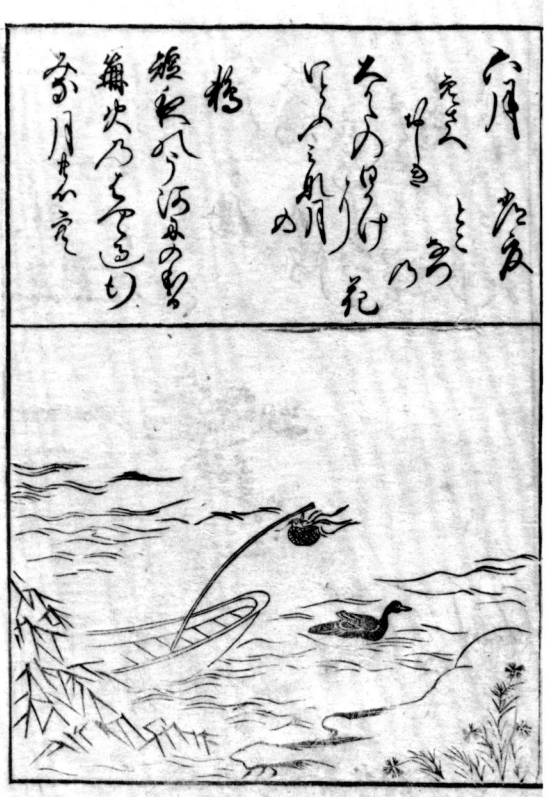

Fig. 19. Artist unknown.
Shigi no hagaki, 1691
(Cat. 7).

Fig. 20. Ogata Kenzan. *Teika's Poems on Flowers and Birds of the Twelve Months*, 1743. Left: The Fourth Month. Right: The Sixth Month (Cat. 10).

Fig. 21. Ogata Kenzan. *Teika's Poems on Flowers and Birds of the Twelve Months*, early-seventeenth-century pottery plates. Left: Third-month poems. Left: Third-month illustration (Cat. 8).

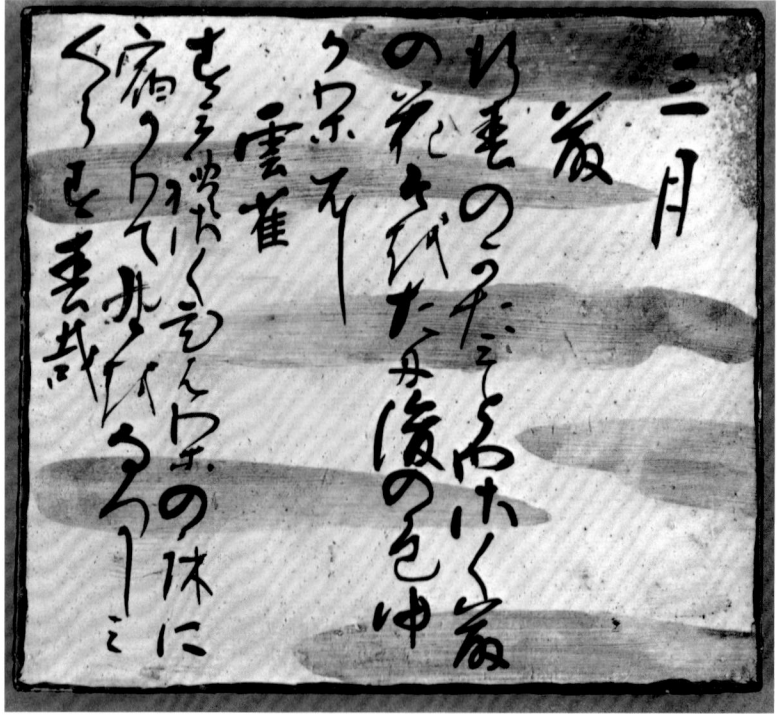

Fig. 22. Kano Tan'yū. *Teika's Poems on Flowers and Birds of the Twelve Months*, 1672 (Cat. 9).

Judging from known works, the last decades of the seventeenth and the first years of the eighteenth centuries marked a high point in the production of paintings on *Teika's Poems on Flowers and Birds*. Soken's Yale screens probably were produced between 1690 and 1692, based on the court ranks of the calligraphers. Similarly, Mitsunari's screens likely date from 1688 to 1710. A handful of minor paintings by lesser-known artists were produced during these same decades.[10] The publication in 1691 of the wood-block printed book *Shigi no hagaki* (A fluttering of snipe's wings) both reflected the popularity of the theme and led to the creation of more paintings of it (Fig. 7; Cat. 19). The title itself is a metaphor for multiple repetition and a cleverly appropriate name for a book printed in numerous copies. The book compiles a wide range of Japanese poems, including *Teika's Poems on Flowers and Birds*. All the poems are accompanied by simple black-and-white pictures that are similar to Tan'yū's and Soken's motifs in general conception, with slight alterations. For example, the picture for the sixth month repeats the half-seen boat emerging from the reeds and the single cormorant of the Michigan painting (Fig. 13), but omits the distant hills and moves the bank of pinks from the lower left- to the lower right-hand corner.

The artist of *Shigi no hagaki* is unknown, although the cover of the edition in the Art Institute of Chicago bears a handwritten attribution to the obscure painter Kaihō Yūsen. Some scholars have postulated a group of lost paintings as the basis for the pictures.[11] In any case, the book greatly contributed to the dissemination and crystallization of the *Teika's Poems of Flowers and Birds* theme and the styles used to depict it.

Shigi no hagaki may well have been owned and admired by Ogata Kenzan (1663–1743). Many of its motifs are repeated in Kenzan's sets of ceramic plates. The best known of these plates is the set in

---

10. Takeno, *Museum* 414 (1985): 7.
11. Nishimoto, *Kokka* 1043 (1981): 27–28.

the MOA Atami Art Museum, dated to 1701 by an inscription on the back of the plate for the twelfth month. As the other sets are close in style, they may also have been produced around this time, early in Kenzan's career as a professional potter. The set of plates in the Los Angeles County Museum of Art (Fig. 21; Cat. 8) recall the Atami set but, curiously, reverse the direction of most of the flower-and-bird motifs. Each square plate features a painting of the flower-and-bird motifs on the inside and has the two poems appropriate to that month written in Kenzan's distinctive calligraphy on the back.

Most of Kenzan's flower-and-bird motifs have more in common with those of *Shigi no hagaki* than with any other extant painted version of the theme. However, a few of the plates display rather novel compositions (for instance, the tenth month shows cranes in flight), and several others are closely related to motifs associated with Tan'yū and Soken. One example, the plate for the fifth month, which shows two water rails but dispenses with the house, uses motifs seen in the Michigan painting and on Soken's Yale screen. On the backs of the plates for the sixth and twelfth months, Kenzan has written the poems exclusively in *Man'yōgana*, the old Japanese system of employing Chinese characters primarily for their sound, instead of the standard Japanese mixture of Chinese characters and Japanese phonetic *kana*. The calligraphy for Soken's seventh-month bird poem in the San Francisco version is also written in *Man'yōgana*. Further study of late-seventeenth- and early-eighteenth-century calligraphy practices may shed some light on the reasons for this use of *Man'yōgana* and its implications. Kenzan, as a student of Soken, surely was exposed to the paintings of his teacher, so it is not surprising that he borrowed ideas as well as motifs from them.

Kenzan's painted plates exhibit the misty atmosphere of Soken's San Francisco paintings and have certain poetic overtones. However, they lack the depth of association that marks Soken's work. The very fact that *Teika's Flowers and Birds* have been

23

painted on plates signals a certain diffusion of the theme. Because here the poems and paintings do not occupy the same picture frame, there is little feeling that the flowers and birds are a visual expression of some layer of meaning in the poems. Instead, the writing of the poems on the back of the plates suggests a game in which one may look at the pictures and then try to recall the poems "hidden" on the underside. Also, the separation of the pictures on twelve plates, which originally would most likely not have been displayed together in sequence, destroys the thematic progress so notable in Soken's paintings. On Kenzan's plates, the twelve flower-and-bird subjects seem more like designs vaguely alluding to a literary theme rather than thoughtful visual explorations of a text.

Teika's Poems on Flowers and Birds continued to flourish as a subject for paintings throughout the eighteenth and early nineteenth centuries. As the subject evolved, being rendered in an ever-increasing number of styles, it lost its poetic core. The meaning of *Teika's Poems* diminished as the subject was gradually subsumed into generic flower-and-bird painting: the process began almost as soon as the theme gained popularity in the 1670s and 1680s. Even in cases where the subject is immediately recognizable, it often seems to be an offhand allusion. In other paintings, the well-established flower-and-bird motifs of *Teika's Poems* are altered or combined in ways that indicate little interest in the literary themes underlying them. Yet it is incorrect to assume that flower-and-bird paintings which do not derive directly from literature have no literary overtones.

For instance, a single six-panel screen of flowers and birds (Fig. 22; Cat. 9) in the Longhi Collection, New York, bearing the signature of Kano Tan'yū at age seventy-one (1672), illustrates no specific literary text but is full of poetic overtones. This screen exhibits a profusion of delicate birds and silky flowers associated with spring and summer.

 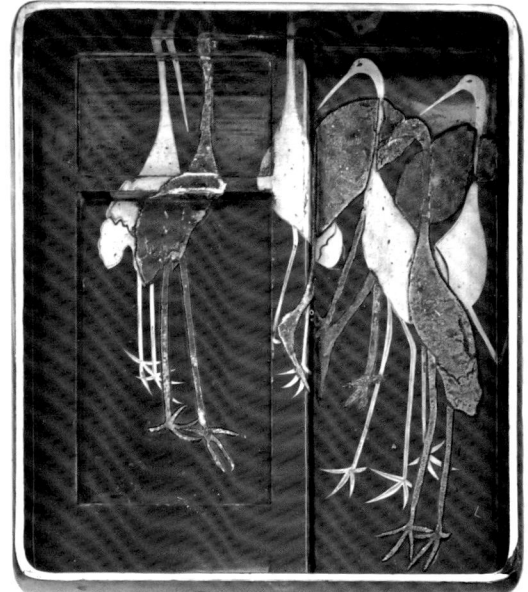

Fig. 23. Mino ware dish, Nezumi Shino type, *Geese in Flight* (Cat. 12).

Fig. 24. Hon'ami Kōetsu. Black-lacquer writing box, *Cranes* (Cat. 11).

Among avian and floral subjects are exotic long-tailed birds, peafowl, herons, a flowering peony, and a pond of lotuses. At the far right, near Tan'yū's signature, a rabbit peeps through a hole in the rock. Tan'yū added to this menagerie several motifs associated with *Teika's Poems on Flowers and Birds*, including a willow with warblers and a pheasant beneath a flowering cherry, as well as cuckoos, plovers, and a flock of cranes in flight. For the sensitive viewer, these details serve as subtle references to the classical literary tradition and contribute another layer of depth to the painting.

While the vast majority of post-seventeenth century paintings of *Teika's Poems on Flowers and Birds* emphasize decorative refinements of the painting surface and delight in the superficial beauty of the flower-and-bird motifs, one set of paintings reexplores the relationship of text and image and visually transforms the implications of the classical subject. In 1743, the eighty-first and last year of his life, Ogata Kenzan made twelve small paintings of *Teika's Poems on Flowers and Birds*. Perhaps originally album leaves, these hanging scrolls are now dispersed among several collections. The paintings of the fourth month and the sixth month (Fig. 20; Cat. 10a–b), both in the Metropolitan Museum of Art, are indicative of the beauty and originality that distinguish the entire set. These radically innovative paintings were produced when, after relinquishing the life of a professional potter in Kyoto, Kenzan was living in Edo as a scholar-artist devoted to reading, writing, and painting. In the last decades of his life, Kenzan created a wealth of simple yet evocative paintings, usually on themes from classical literature, which express his reflective personality.

In these late paintings, Kenzan repeated some basic motifs from his earlier ceramic plates; but the effect is completely original. In violating the order which convention had dictated for the subject, Kenzan created afresh paintings that call forth the evocative power of Teika's poems. Even Kenzan's

25

Fig. 25. Old Imari ware porcelain covered bowl, *Chrysanthemums* (Cat. 16).

Fig. 26. Nonomura Ninsei. Incense container in the shape of a *Wisteria Seedpod* (Cat. 15).

Fig. 27. Kakiemon porcelain headrest, *Quail and Chrysanthemum* (Cat. 13).

earlier plates display the repetitiveness of hackneyed compositions, like the many other eighteenth-century renderings of the theme, but in this painted version, Kenzan abandoned those established models and delved to the essence of his subject. By enlarging the flowers and birds and expanding the text, he filled the entire picture-plane, challenging its artificial limits and making it vibrate with his images. Kenzan's brushwork is refreshingly untrammeled by convention. Its spontaneity suggests the artist's highly personal involvement with his subject. In calligraphy, recalling the energetic and informal script of Teika, Kenzan wrote the two poems for each month literally on the pictures, mingling text and picture, and fusing the poetic images created by the written word with those of painted forms. In the picture of the fourth month, for example, the bird poem begins with the word *hototogisu* (cuckoo) written just below the painted image of that bird. Kenzan's merging of text and picture into a single image is reminiscent of *haiga*—or haiku painting—in which poem and picture similarly are unified rather than splintered, as in the separation of word and image that occurs in the *kasen-e* tradition borrowed by Soken, and in the poem-screen format employed by Mitsunari. In contrast, Kenzan's paintings exhibit the ultimate integration of text and image.

Kenzan harmonized form and content by linking his personal perception—the method of his depiction—with the thing itself—the poetic theme. For him, there was no need to cloak his art in the well-worn garments of a vanished historical past. Rather, to quote from H. D. Harootunian's analysis of Motoori Norinaga, "to recall the ancient exemplars of elegance meant not an affectation or slavish imitation—or even 'pseudo-classicism'—but the power to see and feel, and to connect with others."[12] Kenzan's eventual disregard of the prescribed stylistic norms and constraints created a way of seeing the familiar in an unfamiliar way—in essence, of re-presenting the classical literary experience by representing the very act of poetic creation.

---

12. Harootunian, *Things Seen and Unseen*, p. 116. Much of Harootunian's summation of Motoori Norinaga's philosophy could well describe Kenzan's mature approach to painting.

26

27

Images of the Tales of Ise

Helen Mitsu Nagata

By the seventeenth century, Ariwara Narihira (ca. 825–880) had long been established as the ideal Heian lover and esteemed creator of some of Japan's most beautiful poetry. His legendary status had been defined in part by the appearance of his verse in the early-tenth-century *Kokinshū* and by his inclusion as one of the Thirty-Six Immortal Poets a century later. But it is in the *Tales of Ise* (*Ise monogatari*), a tenth-century poetic narrative, that Narihira really comes alive, especially in mythical episodes describing love affairs with glamorously inaccessible women, such as the imperial consort Fujiwara Kōshi or the high priestess of the Ise Shrine (p. 49).[1] Since the eleventh century, illustrated texts, finely uniting painting, calligraphy, and poetry, have been vital to the transmission of the Narihira legend.

In the seventeenth century, the enthusiasm for *Ise* in Kyoto's highest literary and artistic circles sparked divergent trends in the production of art associated with it. On the one hand, the scholarly pursuits of courtiers and wealthy merchants led to renewed interest in the preservation and transmission of the traditional illustrated text. Examples of this conservative trend can be seen in painted books from the Yale University Beinecke Collection (Fig. 35; Cat. 23) and an album of narrow poem-slip paintings from the Harvard University Art Museums (Fig. 34; Cat. 22). On the other hand, the love of courtiers and wealthy merchants for the *Ise* classic fueled a creative trend toward new pictorial compositions that went beyond illustration to function interpretively, inviting broader contemplation of the poetic tradition. In particular, the pair of six-fold screens attributed to Iwasa Matabei (1578–1650) from the Cleveland Museum of Art (Fig. 42; Cat. 30) and the pair of six-fold screens of Musashi Plain from the Virginia Museum of Fine Arts (Fig. 43; Cat. 31) assume knowledge of the classic and invite the viewer to move quickly beyond the text of a single episode toward contemplation of the fundamental aesthetic of the classical *waka* tradition.

Both trends, the conservative and the creative, can be traced to the Saga-bon (Saga edition) *Ise*, which was probably the single most influential factor in the dissemination of the work during the seventeenth century. The two-volume edition of 1608, printed in moveable type with woodblock illustrations, was the first of several deluxe editions of literary classics published in Saga, near Kyoto. The Saga-bon *Ise* was a collaborative project involving the wealthy merchant and calligrapher Suminokura Soan (1571–1632), the famous tea master, calligrapher, and aesthete Hon'ami Kōetsu (1558–1637), and the court noble and scholar-poet Nakanoin Michikatsu (1556–1610). As the first printed version of *Ise*, it crystallized forty-nine illustrations from the most popular episodes of the *Ise* version compiled by Fujiwara Teika, quickly becoming the authoritative model for subsequent illustrated texts.

Its dissemination, however, encouraged both conservative and creative images of *Ise*. It led to stylistic stagnation in illustrated texts that closely followed the conservative style of the Saga edition; yet at the same time it laid the foundation for new pictorial versions of *Ise* motifs stimulated by increased familiarity with both text and illustration. Moreover, it played an important role in the adaptation of these motifs to decorative arts ranging from textiles and ceramics, such as the Mino ware decorated with the iris motif (Fig. 44; Cat. 32), to fans and lacquerware, such as the three-tiered lacquer box decorated with the autumn grasses motif of Musashi Plain (Fig. 45).

Comparison of a 1608 printed edition of the Saga-bon *Ise* (Fig. 29; Cat. 17b) with a 1629 edition (Fig. 30; Cat. 18b), both from the Spencer Collection of

---

1. All page numbers refer to Helen Craig McCullough, trans., *Tales of Ise: Lyrical Episodes from Tenth-Century Japan* (Stanford: Stanford University Press, 1968). McCullough's translation is based on an edition following a Teika version of this text.

Fig. 28. Tawaraya Sōtatsu. *Tales of Ise*, Mt. Utsu, episode 9 (Cat. 26).

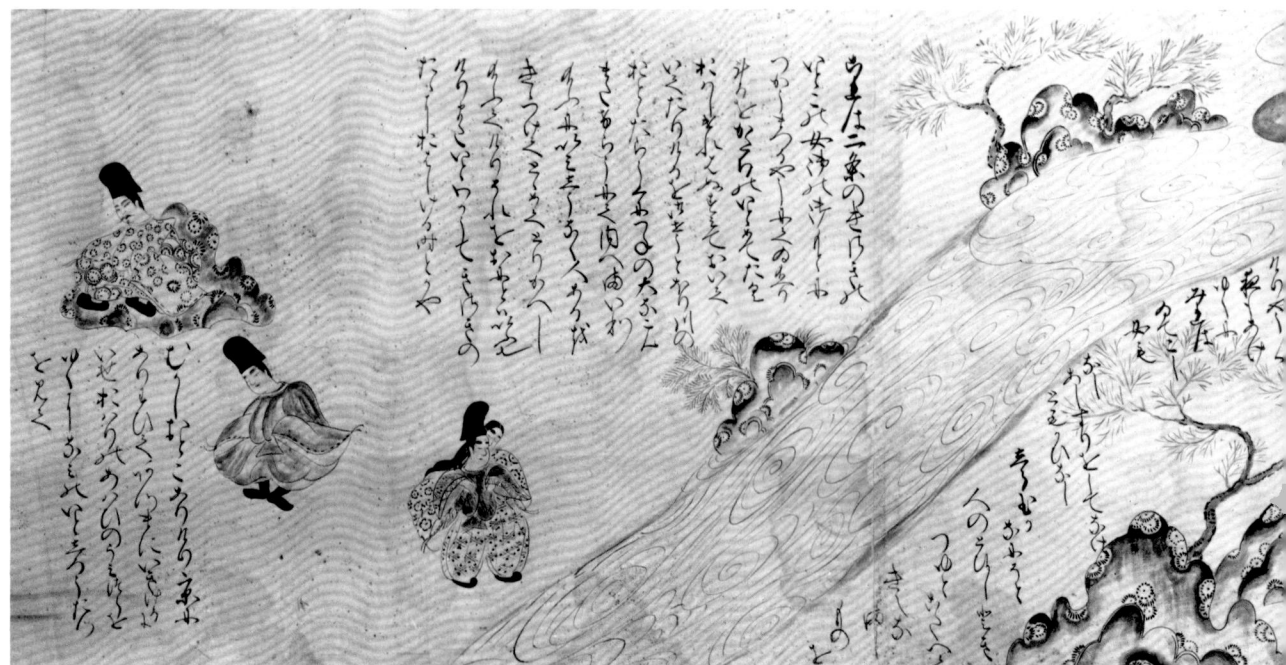

Fig. 32. *Tales of Ise*. From right to left: The Broken Wall, episode 5; Flight along Akuta River, episode 6; and Returning Waves, episode 7. Harvard University Art Museums (Cat. 19).

to display enthusiasm for the classic. In fact, the deluxe manuscript written by the courtier Karasumaru Mitsuhiro (1579–1638), now in the Harvard University Art Museums, was produced about the same time as the 1629 Saga-bon (Fig. 50; Cat. 37). Mitsuhiro's idiosyncratic calligraphy does not merely copy the text but reexpresses it in an unconventional style that seems to dance in space upon the decorated pages.

The Saga books, in essence, condensed and repackaged a centuries-old tradition. Compared to the painted versions that preceded it, the printed Saga-bon is conservative in style and imagery. For example, the late-Muromachi-period monochrome handscroll fragment from the Harvard University Art Museums, now mounted as a hanging scroll, is more expressive in treatment of theme and conveys nuances of feeling through brushwork (Fig. 32; Cat. 19). In a different vein, the late-sixteenth-century set of three small handscrolls from the Spencer Collection creates a vision of refined, gentle simplicity through reduction of compositional motifs and a harmonious color scheme (Fig. 33; Cat. 20).

The Harvard fragment and a section from Scroll 1 of the Spencer handscroll illustrate episodes 5, 6, and 7, a narrative sequence that presumably describes the scandalous love adventure of Narihira and the imperial consort Fujiwara Kōshi. They show, from right to left: the night guards that kept Narihira from visiting Kōshi through a broken wall (the Broken Wall, episode 5); the couple's flight along the Akuta River, where Kōshi came to know what dew is (Flight along Akuta River, episode 6); and Narihira composing a poem of longing on the shore of the Ise Sea (Returning Waves, episode 7). The episodes, fluidly weaving prose and poetry, merge narratives which locate the episodes in a distant time and place, with thirty-one-syllable poems which give them the sparkle and immediacy of human feeling. The poem from the Broken Wall expresses Narihira's frustration (p. 72):

Hito shirenu
Wa ga kayoiji no
Sekimori wa
Yoiyoigoto ni
Uchi mo nenanan.

Would that he might fall asleep
Every night—
This guard
At the secret place
Where I come and go.

In the next episode, the Flight along the Akutagawa, Narihira spirited Kōshi away from her residence. Deciding to rest during a storm, he shel-

tered her in a ruined storehouse, where she was swallowed by a demon while a "thunderclap muffled her screams of terror." When he realized she was gone, Narihira was frantic with grief (pp. 72–73):

Shiratama ka
Nani zo to hito no
Toishi toki
Tsuyu to kotaete
Kienamashi mono o.

When my beloved asked,
"Is it a clear gem
Or what might it be?"
Would that I had replied,
"A dewdrop!" and perished.

Forced to leave the capital because of this scandal, Narihira embarked on a journey eastward. In the next episode, the Returning Waves, he paused to gaze at the white foam of the Ise Sea and was filled with melancholy longing for Kōshi and the capital (p. 74):

Itodoshiku
Sugiyuku kata no
Koishiki ni
Urayamashiku mo
Kaeru nami kana.

How poignant now
My longing
For what lies behind—
Enviable indeed
The returning waves.

In the monochrome fragment, the careful detailing of the face and pose of each figure, such as the slight, sweet smile of the centrally positioned guard in episode 5, or the gentle intimacy of the fleeing couple in episode 6, gives psychological presence to each characterization. The compositions come alive through the expressive power of the artist's brush. In the illustration for episode 6, the swirling Akuta River and the tilt of the ground plane suggest the tumultuous, fearful feelings of the fleeing couple. Moreover, all motifs—the curiously textured rock formations, the clouds shimmering with swashes of mica, the tree shapes, the humorously squat proportions of the figures—are fantastically unreal, fired with the nervous vigor of the artist's hand. Written text and painted image together form diagonal thrusts that lead the eye across the surface, recapturing the poet's emotional rush through chaotic recollections.

The Spencer handscroll illustrations produce a very different expressive effect. Pleasing hues, uncluttered architecture, and smooth ground planes

Images of the "Tales of Ise" 59

33a

33b

33c

Fig. 33. *Tales of Ise*, three small handscrolls. Spencer Collection (Cat. 20).

    a. The Broken Wall, episode 5.
    b. Flight along Akuta River, episode 6.
    c. Returning Waves, episode 7.
    d. The Ise Virgin's Visit, episode 69.
    e. Azusayumi, episode 24.

create a quiet mood. Each component of each scene naturally leads to the next; even the tilted ground plane and the impossibly curled tree trunk in the illustration for the Broken Wall are in pleasant harmony (Fig. 33a). The miniature scale invites intimate contemplation of an idealized, rustic world of the hardworking and lower-stationed. The guards are fully occupied in mundane activities: one diligently fans a fire, a second dozes leaning against the gate post, and a third lies stretched on his mat in full repose. For a brief moment, this illustration tells a simple story of its own, and the viewer forgets Narihira's plight. Similarly, in the illustration of the Returning Waves, the fishermen go about their business in a nonchalant manner, unaware of the beauty of the waves which has so stirred Narihira (Fig. 33c; Cat. 20c). Although the courtiers are larger and more noble in bearing, the fishermen live and work in the same environment, sharing the same world.

On another level, that of literary visualization, both the Harvard and the Spencer scrolls merge perspectives of past and present in poetic images. The narrator's perspective, telling stories set in the past, is fused with that of the poet, bespeaking feelings born of the present. In this way, the illustrations mirror the unique interdependence of prose and poetry within the *Ise* text itself. Conventional compositions of set motifs evolved for each episode, encapsulating this union of narrative past and poetic present. For example, the vital elements of an illustration for the Broken Wall are the sleeping guards by a gate and the broken wall, as seen in Fig. 32 and Fig. 33a. Narihira is sometimes present, yet his presence is not necessary to identify the episode. These conventionalized motifs, isolating only those elements found in both the prose and poetic texts, create frozen moments that unite the past with the present.

Artistic expression, seen in style and imagery, further merges past and present by making more tangible the moment—through characterization, mood, or specific setting—while simultaneously idealizing the present to create an eternal past. For example, the Spencer illustration of the Broken Wall invites the viewer to provide the thoughts that lie behind the simply drawn faces of the guards, individualized by their differing facial features, garments, and poses. The illusion of space allows the viewer to step into the scene and imagine the crackling fire, the still of the night, the earthiness of the wall, and the texture of the straw mats. This combination of images, sensitively arranged and painted, defines an atmosphere that locates the scene in a tangible time and place. At the same time, however, the moment is idealized by the simple elegance of the seated guards, the uncluttered ground planes, and the delicate foliage. The conventional abstraction of cloud and gate motifs moves the scene into a storybook world by linking it to a long tradition of literary illustration. Moreover, beauty is created purely by the formal elements of line, color, and shape. In essence, the artist creates a specific moment only to cast it beyond the grasp of time.

In contrast to the expressive nuance of the Harvard illustrations and the distinct, rustic tranquillity of the Spencer scenes, the expressive effect of the Saga-bon illustrations is subdued. In the Flight along the Akuta River (Fig. 29; Cat. 17a), the Saga-bon picture features monochrome, linear adaptations of traditional *yamato-e* style. Long-standing pictorial conventions are rendered with precise contour lines, uniform textures, and conventional cloud motifs that flatten the composition. For example, in the illustration of the Ise Virgin's Visit (Fig. 29; Cat. 17b), the artist composed the scene with uniform clarity, using architectural divisions exposed by the blown-off roof (*fukinuki yatai*) and depicting his characters in the dash-for-an-eye, hook-for-a-nose (*hikime kagibana*) convention.

The Saga-bon illustrations convey a respect for tradition. They are about the value of the *Ise* classic; they are not about artistic exploration. Partly for this reason, the Saga books became the authoritative model for the majority of subsequent illustrated texts. Similarly, in another classic published in Saga, the *Thirty-Six Immortal Poets*, in the Harvard University Art Museums, the portrait of Narihira reaffirms the cultural significance of the hero of the *Tales of Ise* as the ideal poet (Fig. 31; Cat. 21). One of Narihira's most famous poems is juxtaposed with a monochrome portrait of him posed stiffly in formal court dress, conveying seriousness and emotional detachment. The real drama lies in the emotion of the text, kinetically suggested by the vigorously written characters. After an interminable night spent staring at the plum blossoms and longing for his lost love, Narihira burst into tears and lay on the floor "until the moon sank low in the sky," thinking of the past (p. 71):

Tsuki ya aranu
Haru ya mukashi no
Haru naranu
Wa ga mi hitotsu wa
Moto no mi ni shite.

Is not the moon the same?
The spring
The spring of old?
Only this body of mine
Is the same body. . . .

The poem captures his moment of torment: his recollections of the past, his present misery, and his perception of the relentless cycle of a transitory world. The illustration belies the poem, focusing on the iconic decorum of the poet.

The tendency to illustrate set themes in conventional ways reinforces the iconic image of the classic. Two works that follow this conservative tendency are the set of forty-eight *tanzaku* (poem slips) mounted in an album from the Harvard University Art Museums (Fig. 34) and the set of delicately illustrated books now in the Yale University Beinecke Collection (Fig. 35). Both were probably presented as auspicious gifts on important occasions. Four narrow *tanzaku* from the Harvard album display famous motifs from episode 9, the best-known of *Ise*. They describe Narihira's journey east, begun in episode 7, and are punctuated with poems created at Yatsuhashi, Mt. Utsu, Mt. Fuji, and the Sumida River. Narihira contemplates the irises at a place called Yatsuhashi (Fig. 34a), the ivy and maples at Mt. Utsu (Fig. 34b), the snow on Mt. Fuji (Fig. 34c), and the "capital-birds" frolicking on the Sumida River (Fig. 34d). In each place, the wonders of nature remind Narihira of the great distance he has traveled, the passage of time, and the awesome cyclical persistence of the seasons. Each produces fresh feelings of longing.

In adapting the Saga-bon motifs to the narrow, tall *tanzaku* format, the poem-slip paintings stress the surface beauty of compositional design and rich materials. Comparison of the Yatsuhashi, or "Eight Bridges," scene (Fig. 34a) with the 1629 Saga-bon illustration (Fig. 30) reveals how the artist of the *tanzaku* used the painting medium to adorn the conservative Saga-bon motif. At Yatsuhashi, a place named for eight bridges crossing eight channels of a river, Narihira and his companions seated themselves under a tree for a meal. Inspired by the irises growing in the nearby marshes, Narihira composed a poem, beginning each line with a syllable from the word for iris, *kakitsubata* (pp. 74–75):

Karagoromo
Kitsutsu narenishi
Tsuma shi areba
Harubaru kinuru
Tabi o shi zo omou.

I have a beloved wife,
Familiar as the skirt
Of a well-worn robe,
And so this distant journeying
Fills my heart with grief.

The poem was so moving that the men "all wept onto their dried rice until it swelled with the moisture" (p. 75). The strong design element of the arrangement of courtiers and the zig-zag of wooden bridges on the narrow *tanzaku* format create a static composition, while the gorgeous surface beauty of vivid blues, greens, and multitextured gold bedazzles the eye. It is as if the primary purpose of the illustration were to impress the viewer with sheer brilliance. Accompanying each painting is its corresponding verse from *Ise*, written by a member of the imperial court on poem slips decorated with gold-cloud motifs. Like the Saga-bon illustrations, however, although the *tanzaku* paintings illustrate the text, they are restrained in poetic expression.

In the ensuing Mt. Utsu passage of episode 9 (Fig. 34b), Narihira, facing the gloomy, overgrown path, was filled with fresh longing for his beloved in the capital and asked a wandering ascetic to deliver his message to her (p. 75):

Suruga naru
Utsu no yamabe no
Utsutsu ni mo
Yume ni mo hito ni
Awanu narikeri.

Beside Mount Utsu
In Suruga
I can see you
Neither waking
Nor, alas, even in my dreams.

The artist transformed the dark, forbidding path described in the text into a bold composition of blue-and-green striated land banks shimmering with gold that corresponds little to the mood implied by the text. To a certain degree, the *tanzaku* illustrations echo the expressive restraint found in Narihira's verse, which balances real emotion within elegant poetic style. For those with a knowledge of the classic, poetic pathos lurks beneath the surface of this sumptuous style and conventional imagery. In this sense, the emotional content is dependent on the viewer's understanding of the text, for the illustration itself glosses over the drama of the scene.

The painted books in the Beinecke Collection are a refreshing variation from the conservative group of illustrated texts. The illustration of the Sumida

34d 34c

Fig. 34. *Tales of Ise*, episode 9, paintings and calligraphy on poem slips.
    a. Yatsuhashi.
    b. Mt. Utsu.
    c. Mt. Fuji.
    d. Sumida River.
    Harvard University Art Museums (Cat. 22).

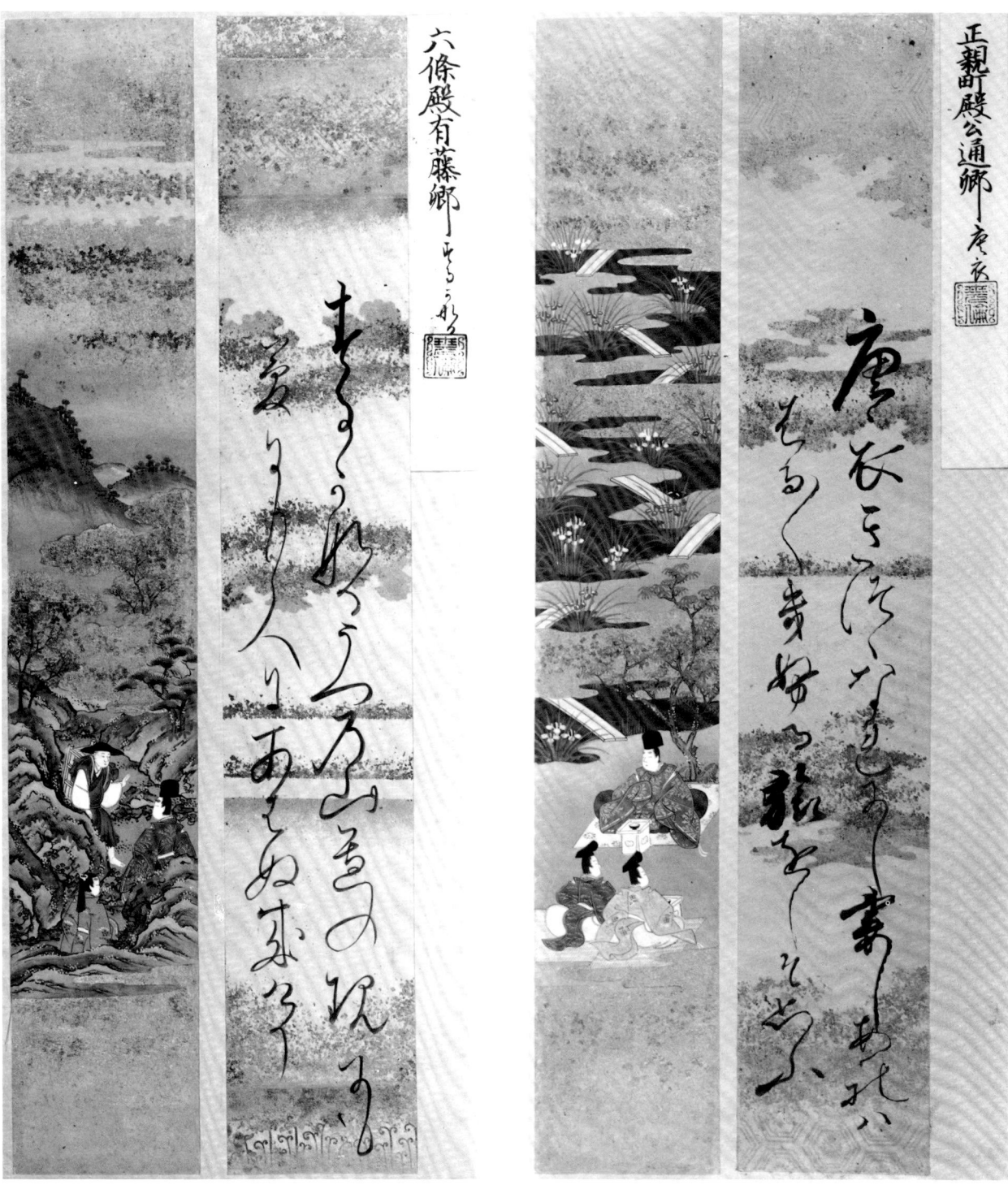

34b　　34a

Images of the "Tales of Ise"　65

35a

35b

River passage of episode 9 virtually reproduces the Saga-bon illustration (Fig. 35a): it presents the same gesturing Narihira, weeping monk, and energetic ferryman in a boat, with birds in the upper left-hand corner. Upon learning from the ferryman that the white birds are called "capital-birds," Narihira recited (p. 76):

> Na ni shi owaba
> Iza koto towamu
> Miyakodori
> Wa ga omou hito wa
> Ari ya nashi ya to.

> If you are what your name implies,
> Let me ask you,
> Capital-bird,
> Does all go well
> With my beloved?

The illustration is playful, set in a bright dreamland of jewel-like hues lined with blue clouds rimmed with white and glimmering with intricate patterns of gold and silver. Tactile lushness, created by the surface beauty of fine applications of translucent light blue and velvet-soft malachite green, complements the quiet lyricism of the rolling water, the uncluttered land mass, the delicate strokes of water and reed motifs, and the expression of each care-fully detailed figure. In addition, the Beinecke illustrations sometimes modernize the conventional Saga-bon motifs with contemporary images, as in the scene from episode 23 (Fig. 35b). This episode describes the love between a man and a woman who "once used to play together beside a well" and eventually married. Much later, the man went to Takayasu, in Kawachi Province, to see a former mistress, but was repulsed when he saw her greedily filling her rice bowl (pp. 87–89). In the Beinecke illustration, the man is peering at his former mistress from behind a fence and has a clear view of her seated in a room adjoining a large kitchen, identifiable by two huge metal pots more typical of dwellings of the Edo period than of Narihira's time.

One of the most completely illustrated surviving texts is a set of four painted books containing 127 illustrations from the Spencer Collection (Fig. 36; Cat. 24). Many of its scenes, such as Narihira's meeting with the Ise Virgin (Fig. 36c), are conventional in style and subdued in expressive effect. The illustrations are not all conservative, however; many creatively incorporate pictorial conventions from landscape painting in order further to aggrandize the importance of Ise. Two illustrations, in par-

Fig. 35. *Tales of Ise*, three painted books. Yale University, Beinecke Collection (Cat. 23).

a. Sumida River, episode 9
b. Former Mistress in Kawachi Province, episode 23
c. Nunobiki Falls, episode 87

ticular—that of the Mt. Fuji passage from episode 9 (Fig. 36a) and that of the emperor's visit to Sumiyoshi (episode 117, Fig. 36b)—present surprising double-page, panoramic landscapes that bring to the texts associations from the genre of *meisho-e*, or famous-place painting.

The Mt. Fuji illustration quickly shifts the viewer's attention from Narihira to the landscape. According to the text, the poet was surprised to see snow on Mt. Fuji at the end of the fifth month and so recited the following poem (pp. 75–76):

> *Toki shiranu*
> *Yama wa Fuji no ne*
> *Itsu tote ka*
> *Ka no ko madara ni*
> *Yuki no fururan.*
>
> Fuji is a mountain
> That knows no seasons.
> What time does it take this for,
> That it should be dappled
> With fallen snow?

Instead of the traditional image of Narihira on horseback turning to look at the famous peak, as in the Harvard *tanzaku* painting (Fig. 34c), here the poet is placed at the right edge of the composition and is nearly lost in a sweeping panorama of Mt. Fuji. Pictorial conventions from landscape painting, such as thatched huts beneath pines, flying geese, and an implied recession through foreground, middle ground, and background, provide us with an idealized vision of rustic tranquillity at the base of Mt. Fuji, one of Japan's most important cultural symbols. Here, the mountain's religious, historic, and literary significance, long celebrated in *meisho-e*, is as much the subject of the painting as the *Ise* episode. Narihira's poem joins with echoes of poems by other poets, lending to the *Ise* classic the great breadth of cultural value associated with the majestic peak.

The Sumiyoshi illustration uses landscape even more boldly to create a new composition for episode 117, rarely illustrated (Fig. 36b). An emperor's journey to Sumiyoshi prompted an exchange of poems between an unidentified poet, possibly Narihira, and the god of Sumiyoshi, patron deity of poetry. The poet wondered at the countless generations of visitors witnessed by the pines at Sumiyoshi beach and was answered by the god (p. 146):

> *Mutsumashi to*
> *Kimi wa shiranami*

36c 36d

Fig. 36. *Tales of Ise*, four painted books. Spencer Collection (Cat. 24).

a. Mt. Fuji, episode 9
b. An Emperor's Visit to Sumiyoshi, episode 117
c. The Ise Virgin's Visit, episode 69
d. Writing on Water, episode 50

Fig. 37-1. Attributed to Tosa Ittoku. *Tales of Ise*. Left: The Broken Wall, episode 5. Right: Returning Waves, episode 7 (Cat. 25).

Mizugaki no
Hisashiki yo yori
Iwaisometeki.

Do you not know
Of the tie that unites us?
Since times as ancient
As my sacred fence
Have I protected you.

The panoramic vision of the Sumiyoshi Shrine brings into the *Ise* narrative a second image associated with the *meisho-e* tradition. Sumiyoshi, famous for the natural beauty of its pines by a white, sandy shore, is also the home of the spirit of the Sumiyoshi pine and, more importantly, the abode of the god of poetry. The grand scene, pictorially reminding the viewer of numerous literary pilgrimages to Sumiyoshi, joins the *Ise* episode in celebrating poetry.

When the formal elements of an *Ise* painting are manipulated to create a new composition that essentially examines the relation between painting and poetic feeling, images frequently become interpretive in function, enriching the *Ise* text with additional meaning. Four album paintings from a set of twelve attributed to Tosa Ittoku (Fig 37; Cat. 25a–d) and four attributed to Tawaraya Sōtatsu, originally from a large set (Figs. 28, 38–41; Cat. 26–

70 *Word in Flower*

29), represent new compositions that adapt traditional *Ise* motifs to explore the expressive potential of painting. The Tosa school artist manipulated the compositional arrangement of settings in order to focus on psychological undercurrents implied by each episode; the Sōtatsu school artist manipulated brushwork and imagery in order to go beyond the literal narrative to appreciate the act of poetic creation.

The Tosa artist explored the expressive possibilities of settings to accentuate moments of high tension. For example, in episode 24, called Azusayumi (a name for a type of wooden bow), a husband returned to his wife after three years in the capital. He knocked on her door, but his wife did not let him in, instead handing him a poem saying she was to wed another man that very night. The husband, outside her closed door, responded before leaving (pp. 89-90):

Azusayumi
Mayumi tsukiyumi
Toshi o hete
Wa ga seshi ga goto
Uruwashimi seyo.

Love your new husband
As I have loved you
All these years.

Images of the "Tales of Ise" 71

Fig. 37-2. Attributed to Tosa Ittoku. *Tales of Ise*. Left: Azusayumi, episode 24. Right: The Ise Virgin's Visit, episode 69 (Cat. 25).

Realizing too late her love for her husband, the wife tried to stop him from leaving by declaring her love, but to no avail. She ran after him in anguish but could not overtake him. Finally, she fell beside a clear spring, traced a poem on a rock with the blood from her finger, and died.

Usually, this episode is illustrated by a picture of the husband pausing outside his wife's house or by a picture of the dying wife inscribing her last verse.[2] The Tosa painting, however, heightens the psychological tension between husband and wife by showing not just the time of the husband's return but the very moment he receives his wife's message (Fig. 37-2). The sliver of space where the husband is sitting suggests the emotional space separating the two. The door, slightly ajar, allows us a glimpse of the husband's bow propped

---

2. The inclusion of a bow (*azusayumi*) identifies the episode but, more interestingly, pictorializes a word that functions in the text as a pillow word (*makura kotoba*), a poetic device described by McCullough as a fixed epithet, normally five syllables long, "thought to invest the poem with an aura of dignity and formality" (p. 13). Although two poems in this episode begin with *azusayumi*, the word is without apparent narrative or symbolic meaning (pp. 213–14). In this illustration, however, it becomes an important pictorial motif.

72 *Word in Flower*

against the wall and draws the eye into the architectural spaces in pursuit of that which is hidden from view. The husband sits with his back to the viewer, yet the tilt of his head suggests the feelings in his heart. The wife is squeezed into a claustrophobic space, locked into place and burdened by the oppressive bulk of her multilayered robes. Her sad face seems to foretell her tragic fate. In these ways, the divisions of space instill the moment with pathos.

The illustration of the Ise Virgin's Visit (episode 69) also uses architectural setting to express the essential feeling of the poem (Fig. 37-2). In contrast to the tragic mood of episode 24, however, this painting creates a mood of gentle intimacy. Whereas the Azusayumi scene juxtaposes confined architectural depth with impenetrable flatness to express the psychological tension between husband and wife, in this painting recession into pictorial space allows the Ise Virgin to move easily into the small, intimate chamber where Narihira awaits in anticipation, suggesting their intimacy. The composition underscores Narihira's desire by placing the coy Ise Virgin just at the entrance of the half-open doors, drawing attention to the pending moment of passage. Comparison of this image with the tranquil atmosphere created in a painting of the same epi-

Fig. 38. Tawaraya Sōtatsu. *Tales of Ise*. Visit to Sumiyoshi, episode 68 (Cat. 27).

sode from Scroll 2 of the Spencer handscrolls (Fig. 33d; Cat. 20d) reveals how much the manipulation of setting and space can accentuate the psychological tension of captured moments filled with unspoken feelings.

The Tosa paintings illustrating the Broken Wall (Fig. 37-1; Cat. 25a) and Returning Waves (Fig. 37-1; Cat. 25b) create physical outdoor spaces that reveal the poet's state of mind. The emphatic placement of the tree in the exact center of the scene of the Broken Wall forms another barrier, in addition to the guards, between Narihira and the woman he desires to visit. Forced to turn away, Narihira is left alone with his sadness. The tree makes more tangible the sense of isolation central to the episode.

In Returning Waves, the natural setting surrounds the courtiers and isolates them as though on an island. The tilted ground plane of the water and the diagonal slant of the thin shoreline that separates the courtiers from the water create a sense of instability which reinforces the idea of change suggested by the poem. Feeling isolated from loved ones and longing for the past, Narihira envies the returning waves that roll in to shore and out again, while he must travel on, away from home. Even more subtly, the sense of wind blowing through

74 Word in Flower

Fig. 39. Tawaraya Sōtatsu. *Tales of Ise*. The Sacred Fence, episode 71 (Cat. 28).

the courtiers' robes suggests the evanescence of life, which underlies the poet's melancholy.

While the Tosa paintings magnify the psychological moment in compositions that probe the depths of feeling in individual episodes, the Sōtatsu album leaves create a new expressive effect that fuses poetry and painting with a beauty and energy of its own. This approach is seen in four album leaves: the Mt. Utsu scene from episode 9 in the Burke Collection (Fig. 28; Cat. 26); Narihira at the Sumiyoshi Shrine, episode 68, from the Cleveland Museum of Art (Fig. 38; Cat. 27); the Sacred Fence, episode 71, from the Nelson Gallery (Fig. 39; Cat. 28); and Nunobiki Falls, episode 87, from the Minneapolis Institute of Art (Fig. 40; Cat. 29). Essentially, each painting alludes to the illustrative tradition of *Ise* in order to depict it anew. The artist manipulates both formal elements and illustrative motifs to create a new lyricism that brings allusions from the past into the present.

The Mt. Utsu scene from episode 9 well illuminates the layers of effects that characterize each album leaf. Formal elements, poetic imagery, and calligraphy are masterfully combined to create a unified expression. Each shape, especially those textured with the wet puddling of colors charac-

Fig. 40. Tawaraya Sōtatsu. *Tales of Ise*. Nunobiki Falls, episode 87 .(Cat. 29).

teristic of the Sōtatsu style, and each fluid touch of the brush transmits a sense of process that recreates the generative moment of artistic creation. While the zig-zag motif of the path suggests pictorial recession into space, the path is also boldly flattened, drawing attention to the surface beauty of the luscious hues of mineral color, the luminous gold, and the flow of curvilinear contours. The formal elements are dynamic, reflecting the artist's delight in balancing spontaneity with precise control of the medium and contrasting illusions of pictorial space against the flatness accentuated by surface beauty. The painting tempts the viewer to lose himself in the lyricism of surface effects, and to linger awhile in a timeless world where past becomes present as he experiences the spontaneity of painting.

The Mt. Utsu painting also subtly modifies the traditional illustrative motifs to bring new meaning to the painting. Figural motifs adopted from other illustrated classics add layers of literary allusions to the image. As Yamane Yūzō has shown, the figure of the ascetic echoes that of Priest Saigyō at the shore of the Ise Sea in a copy Sōtatsu made of the *Tales of Saigyō* in 1630, while the figure of Narihira

Fig. 41. Tawaraya Sōtatsu. *Tales of Ise*. Mt. Utsu, episode 9, detail (Cat. 26).

Fig. 42. Scenes from the Tales of Ise.
    a. Detail of right screen: Yatsuhashi, episode 9.
    b. Detail of right screen: The Well Curb, episode 23.
The Cleveland Museum of Art (Cat. 30).

42b

Images of the "Tales of Ise" 79

Fig. 43. *Musashi Plain*. Virginia Museum of Fine Arts (Cat. 31).

resembles a courtier in the *Kitano tenjin engi* (Legend of Sugawara no Michizane).³ These two illustrated classics are particularly important, as they describe the legendary lives of two of Japan's most beloved literary personages. Saigyō (1118–1190), the semi-reclusive poet-monk, was famed for his deep love of nature, while the courtier-poet Sugawara no Michizane (845–903) was worshipped as the god of literature and calligraphy. The figure of the ascetic immediately recalls the story of Saigyō, who made many pilgrimages, composing poems wherever he went. The allusion to the poet-monk not only brings to *Ise* associations of Saigyō's love for nature and his sensitivity to man's fleeting existence, but also emphasizes the close relationship between poetry and Japan's famous places in the *meisho-e* painting tradition. In essence, the visual quotation of the poet-monk from the *Tale of Saigyō* functions like a pictorial *honka dori*, the *waka* technique of echoing a phrase from a famous poem, placing it in a new context to enrich the new poem. Thus, by alluding to Saigyō, the album painting brings the past into the present, adding depth to the new *Ise* illustration.

The fact that the poems are written on the painting itself further accentuates the layers of overlapping expression shared by the formal elements and illustrative motifs. Not only does the verse literally correspond to the illustration, but the dynamic tension of the written characters also echoes the technical effect of the painted motifs. The painting heightens a sense of the creative flow of poetry-making that transforms emotions into words and images. It fuses painting, calligraphy, and poetry: it adds an increased sense of poetry to the painted motif, of visual beauty to the poetry, and of the creative impetus that underlies the literary arts. In contrast to the conservative *tanzaku* painting of the same episode (Fig. 34b) which flattens space and defines the motifs with a crystalline hardness, the Sōtatsu painting creates an expansive space that breaks new ground in its strong sense of evolving lyricism.

---

3. The version Sōtatsu copied was based on a 1500 version painted by Kaida Umenenosuke Tomoyasu. The Narihira figure is similar to a courtier in scroll 5 of a set in the Imperial Collection. Yamane Yūzō also links the motif of the horse and attendant in the lower right of the composition to a similar motif from the *Tale of the Hōgen War*. Yamane Yūzō, "Den Sōtatsu hitsu *Ise monogatari zu no senmen*, byōbu shikishi," *Sōtatsu-ha* 1, p. 40.
4. According to Yamane Yūzō, one set of album leaves was very likely commissioned by Ogata Sōken's mother, Ichijuin (the second wife of Sōhaku, Hon'ami Kōetsu's nephew), who may have planned the album to celebrate her son's coming of age and, more importantly, to establish relations between her son and the circle at Takagamine of which Kōetsu was the center.

These four album leaves were originally from a much larger set. While each leaf is like a poem in itself, the set as a whole must have resembled an anthology of visualized poems with its own theme: a celebration of the timeless joy that exists in the spontaneity and truthfulness of poetry. With this, the Sōtatsu album leaves offer a new interpretation of the Ise classic as a poetic work with universal relevance. Moreover, they reflect the enthusiasm for classical poetry among the literary circles of courtiers and wealthy merchants who inscribed the poems and enjoyed the works.[4]

Containing neither written text nor inscribed poems, the pair of folding screens from the Cleveland Museum of Art (Fig. 42; Cat. 30) and those of *Musashi Plain* from the Virginia Museum of Fine Arts (Fig. 43; Cat. 31) are dependent on the viewer's knowledge of the illustrative tradition for recognizing the literary allusions. These screens exemplify two ways in which the whole illustrative tradition of the *Tales of Ise* could be cited in compositions that reflect a modern seventeenth-century celebration of it.

The Cleveland screens visualize *Ise* in its entirety—in fact, at a single glance. About twenty episodes are roughly organized into two groups, with earlier episodes on the right screen and later on the left. Rather than "reading" the narrative of the episodes, the seventeenth-century viewer could take pleasure in recollecting well-known scenes randomly continuing from one to the next. Even while one is viewing a single part, one is conscious of the whole. To be sure, the screens were meant to be enjoyed through close scrutiny, scene by scene. The easily recognizable episodes create melodrama by emphasizing active gestures and strong facial expressions. In the Yatsuhashi scene from episode 9 (Fig. 42a) Narihira, his friends, and his attendants strike exaggerated poses while they weep.

Although each figural motif is from a different episode with a distinct time and place, all share the same ground plane and setting. In the detail of a boy and girl playing beside the well curb, from episode 23 (Fig. 42b), only a single straw fence separates the children from motifs of two different episodes. The screens, in a sense, mimic the literary nature of the text itself, stringing together a series of distilled units into a disjointed narrative. In like fashion, the Cleveland screens create a whole vision of the *Tales of Ise* from a collection of pictures. Moreover, the use of gold cloud both to divide the scenes and to unite the composition horizontally creates splendor that animates the overall design and proclaims a celebratory attitude toward the *Ise* text.

44

Fig. 44. Mino ware, Ki-Seto type, dining dishes (mukōzuke) with designs of Iris (Cat. 32).

Fig. 45. Three-tiered lacquer box for food (jūbako) with motifs of Musashi Plain (Cat. 33).

While the Cleveland screens treat the *Ise* theme as the sum of its diverse parts, the *Musashi Plain* screens recall the dominant mood of *Ise* by poetic evocation of a single motif. In this way, they allude to the classic in the same way as the famous pair of Iris screens by Ogata Kōrin allude to the Yatsuhashi passage of episode 9.[5] The *Musashi Plain* screens, however, conflate several themes. On one level, they refer to the famous episode 12 of *Ise*, in which a man and his lover hid among the grasses only to be discovered when officials threatened to burn them out. The woman, fearing for her lover's life, recited (p. 78):

Musashino wa
Kyō wa na yaki so
Wakakusa no
Tsuma mo komoreri
Ware mo komoreri.

Do not set fire today
To Musashi Plain,
For my beloved husband
Is hidden here,
And so am I.

---

5. For reproduction of the Iris screens by Ogata Kōrin, see Kōno Motoaki, ed., *Nihon bijutsu kaiga zenshū 17: Ogata Kōrin* (Tokyo: Shūeisha, 1976), no. 13.

However, the screens also carry broader associations of the place—both within the poetry and the *meisho-e* traditions. Musashi Plain, long paired with the autumn moon or with Mt. Fuji in classical poetry, is evocative of man's isolation, the awesome vastness of nature, and the transitoriness of life in this world. In pairing Musashi Plain with the silvery autumn moon in the right screen and with Mt. Fuji in the left, the screens allude to both poetic traditions. Each screen, however, essentially juxtaposes two nature motifs: the painting has no obvious narrative. Rather, the two screens create an imaginary space pregnant with poetic mood. By contrasting the fleeting beauty of the moon, dimly seen hugging the lower edge of the right screen, with the monumental permanence of Mt. Fuji, which looms to the upper edge of the left, the overall composition heightens a sense of the wide expanse between. At the same time, the haunting moon and the majestic peak are united in one image. Both are set against a sea of delicate autumn flowers and seen through a prism of waving grasses in a way that accentuates the poetic lyricism uniting the two. The viewer becomes the poet who provides the text and meaning for the painting. The painting is in effect an emblem of the past which, by inspiring active recollection, returns the past to the present.

45

Past and Present, Text and Image

Carolyn Wheelwright

On the eleventh day of the eleventh month of Keichō 11 (1606), Hon'ami Kōetsu inscribed a melancholy autumn poem from the *Shin kokinshū* on a poetry sheet, or *shikishi*, that had been decorated with springtime cherry blossoms in the painting studio of Tawaraya Sōtatsu (Fig. 47; Cat. 34). This small *shikishi*, one of sixteen known today that carry Kōetsu's seal and the unusual date, may have been made to honor Konoe Nobutada, who stepped down from his high court position of Senior Regent on that day. Quite likely, it was part of a set of thirty-six such cards displayed on a pair of folding screens, a format frequently employed for commemorative or festive occasions.[1] In its creators and its probable social occasion, in its format and its medium, its style and its visual and verbal references, this small poetry sheet in the Metropolitan Museum of Art embodies the genius of the artistic renaissance that swept through the Kyoto region in the late-sixteenth and early-seventeenth century. Signs of revival were everywhere, as the imperial capital was rebuilt following the chaos of more than a century of civil war. Activities leading to renewal of court traditions were particularly notable among Kyoto's artists and craftsmen.

Nobutada, Kōetsu, and Sōtatsu were part of a creative alliance of courtiers, artisans, and wealthy townsmen of the Kyoto region who were reaffirming their continuity with the classical past. For a range of political, social, and artistic reasons, these men, like Hosokawa Yūsai and Karasumaru Mitsuhiro (see "The Past in the Present"), were drawn to the refined aesthetic traditions of the imperial court. They plumbed the courtly past for text and image, for verbal and visual material to use in creating a rich sensory expression of their own present. Their present, the Keichō era (1596–1615), was a vibrant age when Kyoto's famous artists and craftsmen were producing, in increasing numbers, works of calligraphy, painting, ceramic, lacquer, metalwork, and textiles—all manner of material culture.

Kōetsu, by profession a connoisseur and sharpener of swords, was an elite townsman, a craftsman whose cultural circle included high ranking courtiers such as Konoe Nobutada, as well as esteemed craftsmen-artists such as Sōtatsu. Kōetsu was steeped in the aesthetic world of the tea ceremony and was recognized as one of the greatest calligraphers of his age. He collaborated with Suminokura Soan in producing the Saga-bon *Ise* in 1608, providing the model for the linked phonetic script used in its printing (see above, pp. 54–57). He made designs for ceramic and lacquer wares (Fig. 24; Cat. 11), and directed paper makers, decorators, and painters to create the visual grounds on which he could write his calligraphy. Kōetsu frequently ordered decorated *shikishi* and handscrolls from Sōtatsu, who also maintained close connections with wealthy merchants and skilled craftsmen, especially those involved in the city's flourishing textile industry in the Nishijin area of Kyoto.

This catalogue, like the works of art it presents and interprets, was a collaborative venture: each of the four authors owes ideas and interpretations to each of the others. Nevertheless, my debt to James Ulak must be acknowledged in particular, for initially the final essay was to be a joint project. Many of the ideas and words in "Past and Present, Text and Image" are direct quotations from discussions we had or from memos passed between us, and the essay is much richer for that exchange.

In addition, I wish to acknowledge the contribution of Chung-lan Wang, whose seminar paper on Kōetsu's calligraphy provided the starting point for this essay.

1. A pair of six-panel screens bearing decorated poetry cards with calligraphy in Kōetsu's elegant style is in the Freer Gallery of Art and is published in Fu, Lowry, and Yonemura, *From Concept to Context*, no. 29, pp. 88–89. A well-known set of thirty-six *shikishi* bearing poems from the *Shin kokinshū* in the Museum für Ostasiatische Kunst, Berlin, is thought to have been mounted on folding screens; see Yamane, ed., *Rinpa*, pls. 17–25.

Fig. 46. *Flowering Cherry and Autumn Maple with Poem Slips*, detail (Cat. 48).

Fig. 47. Calligraphy by Hon'ami Kōetsu and underpainting attributed to Tawaraya Sōtatsu. *Autumn Poem on Cherry Blossoms*, dated 1606 (Cat. 34).

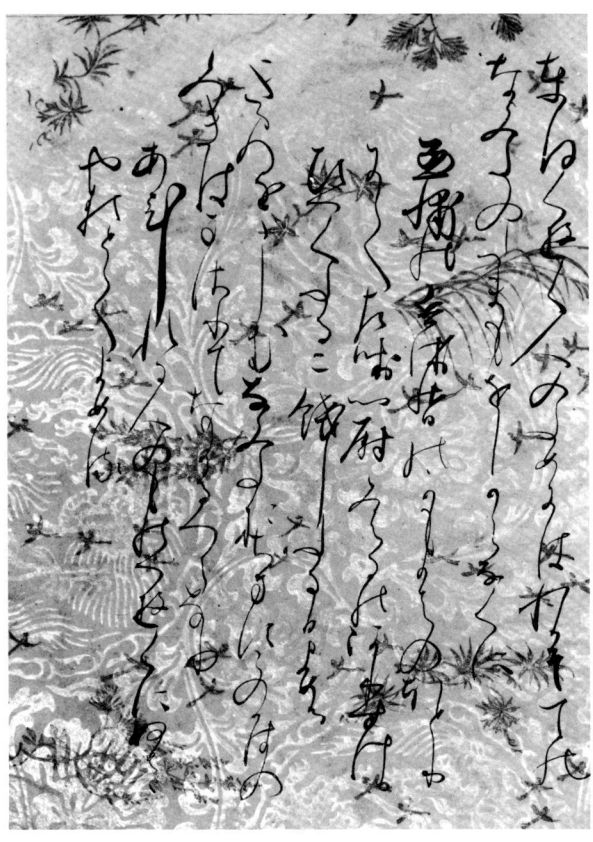

Fig. 48. Fujiwara Sadanobu. *Poems from the Tsurayuki-shū*, ca. 1112 (Cat. 35).

The Metropolitan *shikishi* of the eleventh year of Keichō is eloquent testimony to the reuse of the aesthetic past by Kōetsu and Sōtatsu as they created the resonant aesthetic of their present. It attests to their identification with an ongoing courtly tradition that has many points of reference in the past, each with its own connotations. While the literary allusion of the *shikishi* is to an early-thirteenth-century poem from the imperially sponsored *Shin kokinshū*, the dominant visual source can be found in earlier, twelfth-century court productions of *waka* poetry written in *kana*, the phonetic Japanese script, on a variety of sumptuously decorated paper. Some of these luxurious albums and scrolls of decorated calligraphy became accessible to a larger cross-section of society when, as a result of the social upheavals of war in the sixteenth century, they were released from the closed world of the imperial court. One such exquisite production is represented by a fragment in the Burke Collection from the *Tsurayuki-shū*, one of the decorated calligraphy albums of the *Thirty-Six Immortal Poets*, thought to have been offered as a magnificent gift in honor of the sixtieth birthday of Retired Emperor Shirakawa in the third month of 1112 (Fig. 48; Cat. 35).

The page in the Burke Collection presents a vibrant, multilayered surface. Smooth white paper forms the ground for layers of flowing decoration: an overall design of playful lions cavorting in double-vine scrolls printed in mica, a scattering of flying birds, maple leaves, pine branches, and heads of pampas grass painted in silver, lines of swirling, twisting, dancing *kana*, written in rich black ink by Fujiwara Sadanobu (1088–1156), one of the foremost calligraphers of his age. The relaxed movement of the linked phonetic script produces an elegant effect of spontaneity and ease against the warm shimmer of mica and the sparkle of silver. It was just such a lavish aesthetic program that provided Kōetsu and Sōtatsu with a rich foundation for their expressions of material abundance.

The thirty-nine luxurious albums of the *Thirty-Six Immortal Poets* were presented by the court to the temple of Nishi Hongan-ji of Kyoto in 1549, and late-sixteenth-century journals indicate that pages from the set were being displayed for appreciation during tea ceremonies.[2] Kōetsu and Sōtatsu could

---

2. Tamamushi, *Bijutsushi* 117, p. 70, n. 37 on p. 74, citing Kyūso Hitaku, *Nishi Hongan-ji bon Sanjūrokuninshū seisei* (Tokyo: Kazama Shobō, 1966), p. 76, and n. 38 on p. 74, citing the *Tokitsune-kyō ki*.

Fig. 49. Shōkadō Shōjō. Left: *Hollyhocks*. Right: *Clematis* (Cat. 36).

have seen them, and they surely knew similar works. Kōetsu collected examples of earlier calligraphy he admired and undoubtedly owned at least one piece of twelfth-century *kana* calligraphy on a decorated ground. Nevertheless, Kōetsu and Sōtatsu probably would not have considered their own creation of decorated poetry sheets in 1606 as a renaissance of twelfth-century courtly art. Rather, they would have viewed their collaboration as a modern expression of a continuing aesthetic tradition associated with the imperial court.

The Metropolitan *shikishi* clearly owes its conception to earlier works such as the *Thirty-Six Immortal Poets* album. Nevertheless, there is a fundamental difference between the delicate layers of decoration on the surface of the twelfth-century page and the dynamic interaction of written text and silhouetted image on the poetry sheet of 1606. It is the difference between a past prescribed by the decorum of the imperial court and a present formed by the remarkable aesthetic alliance of courtier and townsmen. Sōtatsu's frontal cherry blossoms stem from long-standing tradition, but these enlarged silver flowers are bold fragments of a larger tree, truncated by the frame of the poetry sheet. Sliding among the blossoms are clouds of gold, their irregular contours inserting an ambiguous echo by recalling the traditional sand-island motif that identifies ocean waters. This is a modern magnification of floral motifs painted in the sheer material glory of gold and silver.

Against this ground, and communicating with it,

Kōetsu wrote a melancholy autumn *waka* by Kamo no Chōmei (1155?–1216):

*Nagamureba chiji ni mono omou aki ni mata
wagami hitotsu no mine no matsukaze*

As I sit staring in this autumn with thousands of
  sad thoughts,
here, too, the pine wind from the mountain, for
  myself alone.
  — Translation by Edward Kamens

Kōetsu's *kana* writing style emulates the princely tradition represented by Sadanobu's calligraphy on the Burke page from the *Tsurayuki-shū*. The fine lines of his *kana*, however, are punctuated with emphatic Chinese characters, or *kanji*, which owe their flourish to the intervening tradition of Chinese calligraphy that had been dominant during the fifteenth and sixteenth centuries in Japan. Kōetsu's revival of early *kana* calligraphy, therefore, was not a simple return to a past courtier's style. His calligraphy was a new synthesis, enriched by his understanding of Chinese traditions more recently practiced in Japan.

This *shikishi* is not the work of one artist. Like Sadanobu's calligraphy on the mica-printed, silver-painted paper, Kōetsu's writing is part of a richly evocative decorative ensemble. It is a collaborative work with multiple parts created by a poet, a paper maker, a designer, and a calligrapher. Kōetsu, the final performer in this creative process, demonstrated his sensitive awareness of both the text and the image in his handling of the rhythmic accents of his calligraphy.

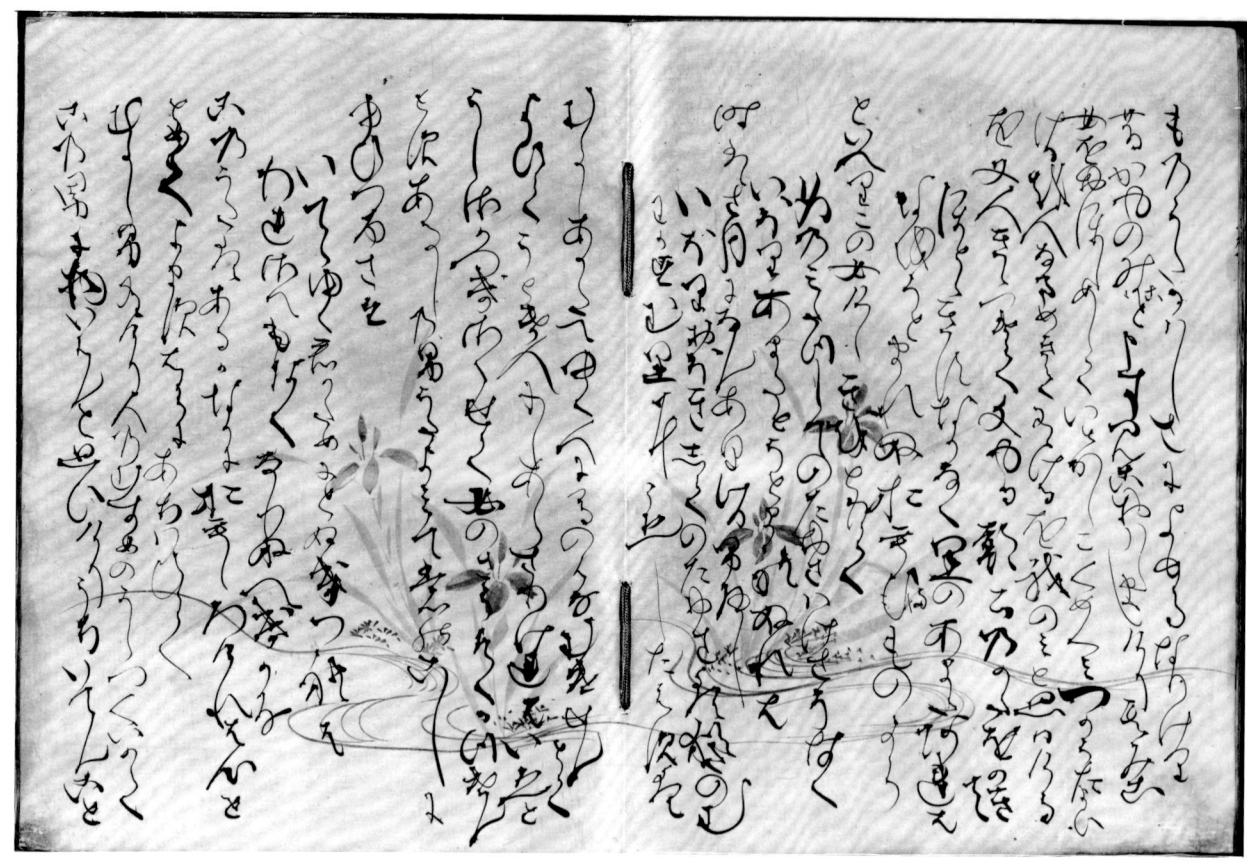

Fig. 50. Karasumaru Mitsuhiro. *Tales of Ise*, ca. 1630 (Cat. 37).

Most dramatic is the interplay between Kōetsu's corpulent Chinese characters and Sōtatsu's silver cherry blossoms. The fleshy first character, *naga[mureba]* ([as I] stare), swirls adroitly in front of a lush silver blossom and a silver-edged cloud jutting into the upper right corner of the sheet. At the bottom of the second line, *aki* (autumn) originally stood out against the mass of silver blossoms, but today tarnish obscures the contrast. Pirouetting theatrically in the exact center of the sheet, the two characters for *wagami* (myself) are the boldest of all. They function much as potent Sanskrit letters in the center of a Buddhist mandala do, here compelling us to focus on the subjective persona of Chōmei's reflective poem. Finally, against a relatively open area of cloud at the top of line four, the Chinese character for "mountain peak," *mine*, is thinner and sharper, suggesting the chill loneliness of the mountainous source of the wind, *kaze*, which is written unstably at the bottom of that line, as fleeting as the element it names.

There is little doubt that Kōetsu was responding both to the meaning of the poem and to the floral composition on the sheet, personalizing his response to the poetic expression of Kamo no Chōmei and carrying forward the visual creative process initiated by Sōtatsu. Clearly, the fact that Kōetsu wrote an autumn poem on a spring image does not imply that he ignored the meaning of the seasons while concerning himself only with the interplay of visual design.[3] Rather, it suggests that this superimposition was part of his artistic concept, which provides an important key to understanding the courtly aesthetic that was sought by the sophisticated circle of courtiers and townsmen in the Kyoto region during the first half of the seventeenth century.

---

3. There are many examples of disagreement of season in the text of calligraphy and the motif decorating its ground, both in the twelfth-century Nishi Hongan-ji *Thirty-Six Immortal Poets* and in seventeenth-century decorated calligraphic works. Many of these probably resulted from disinterest in aligning the seasons; but clearly many, like Kōetsu's Metropolitan poetry sheet, are conscious choices to add nuances of meaning.
4. See Stinchecum, *Kosode*, cat. 2–6.

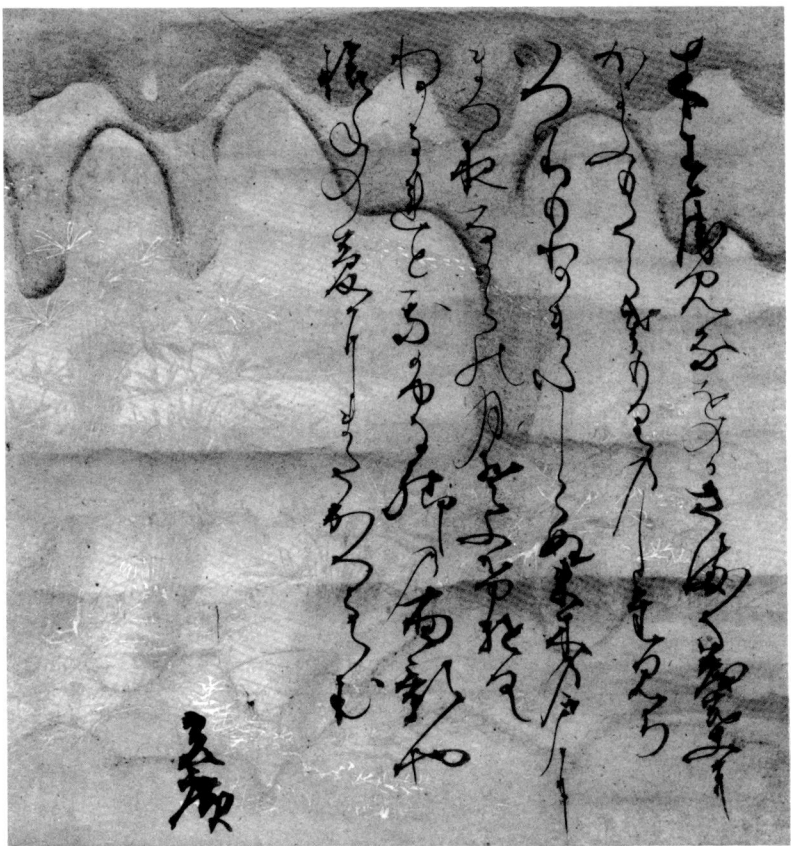

Fig. 51. Karasumaru Mitsuhiro. *Three Poems* (Cat. 38).

Kōetsu and his colleagues took pleasure in creating new wholes by juxtaposing undisguised fragments from the allusive past—the visual equivalent of the poetic technique of *honka dori*, or allusive variation (see above, p. 22). Just as Hosokawa Yūsai abstracted elements from various aesthetic traditions, reusing them in new combinations that echoed the creative processes of Fujiwara Teika and other poets of the early-thirteenth century, so Sōtatsu and Kōetsu restructured visual imagery from the past. On the Metropolitan *shikishi*, Sōtatsu appropriated silver cherry blossoms and billowing gold clouds/sand spits from the long tradition of nature imagery for spring, but magnified them and brought them close to the surface of the poetry sheet, allowing them to be radically truncated by the edges of the format. Sōtatsu, therefore, provided Kōetsu with a dense surface of allusive fragments that continues beyond the frame left and right, top and bottom.

When Kōetsu wrote Kamo no Chōmei's autumn poem on this decorated spring ground, he created a palpable tension, both visual and verbal. Visually, the rhythmic contrasts of tensile Japanese *kana* and resonant Chinese *kanji* allow the two calligraphic traditions to interact, and the dynamic movement of written words plays against truncated patterns of blossoms and clouds. Verbally, the melancholy thoughts in Chōmei's autumn poem reiterate the transience of beauty in the visual image of fleeting spring blossoms, a poignant image for Nobutada, a courtier retiring from the worldly pinnacle of the highest court position attainable. The whole is boldly contemporary, produced in a dynamic age of peace and material abundance, dense with thick strands and thin filaments of ink interacting with a glorious surface of gold and silver patterns that recall nothing so much as the brilliant brocades that were being produced in the Nishijin district of Kyoto during the Keichō years.[4]

Two poetry sheets by Shōkadō Shōjō in the Metropolitan Museum of Art, *Hollyhock* and *Clematis*, reflect the same creative principle of juxtaposition of fragments to create a new whole (Fig. 49). Shōkadō, a Shingon monk of the Shinto shrine of Iwashimizu Hachimangū in southwest Kyoto, is

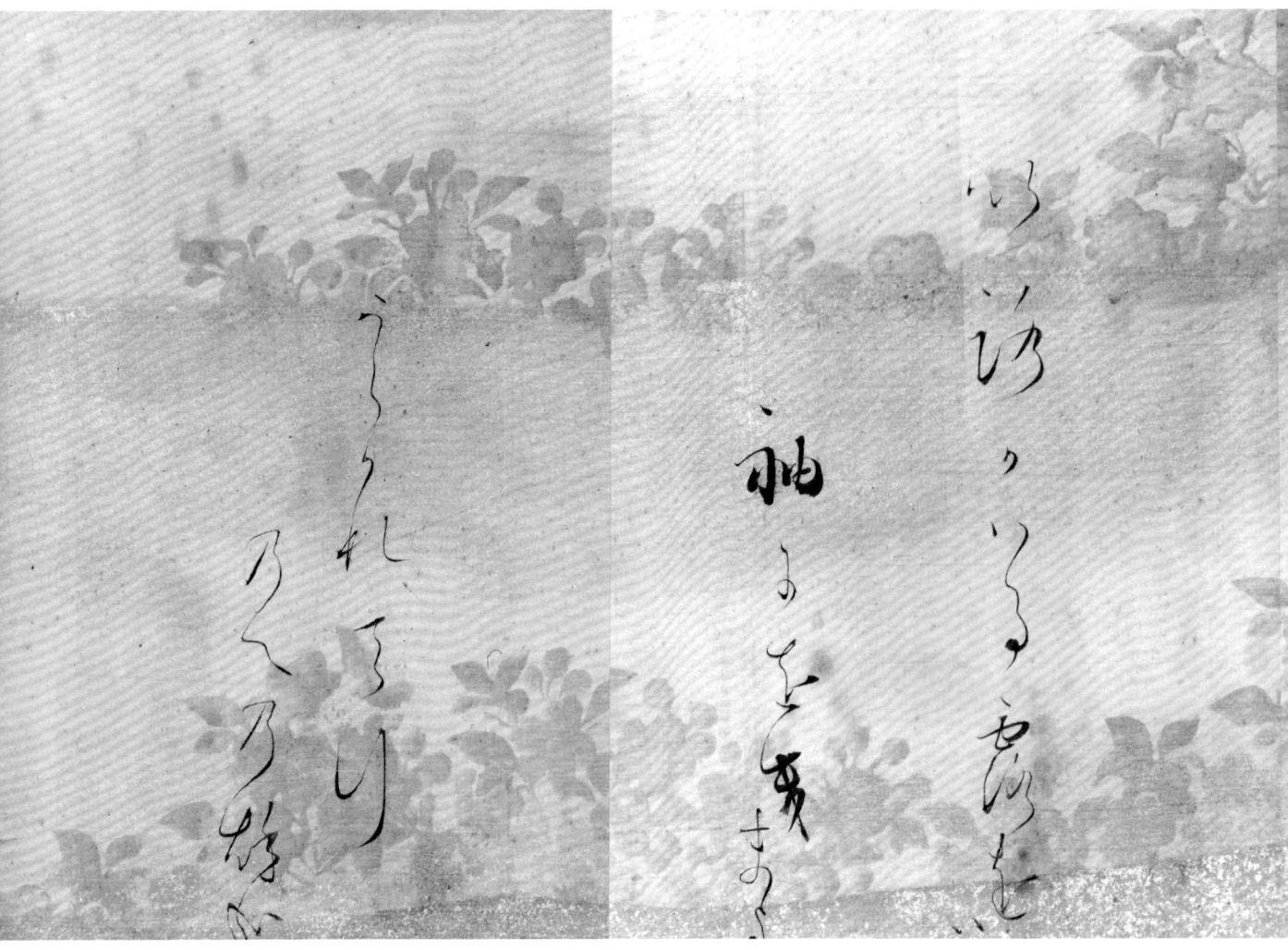

Fig. 52. Calligraphy by Hon'ami Kōetsu, printed design by a follower of Sōtatsu. *Twelve Poems from "Shin kokinshū"*, opening section (Cat. 40).

ranked with Kōetsu and Konoe Nobutada as one of the three best calligraphers of his age.[5] Shōkadō also looked to the courtly tradition of *kana* calligraphy for inspiration.

These poetry sheets, roughly contemporary with the Kōetsu-Sōtatsu *shikishi*, nonetheless provide a more relaxed, less sumptuous, aesthetic experience. The gold and silver floral motifs are larger in relation to the format, and less dense, but they, too, extend beyond their borders, giving a sense of continuation. On one *shikishi* (Fig. 49; Cat. 36a), two silver hollyhock blossoms at the top of their vertical stalk are contained within the frame, while a neighboring stalk with a few golden leaves bends into the upper right-hand corner. The sturdy lines of the stems capture the hardy nature of these summer flowers, while on the other poetry sheet (Fig. 49; Cat. 36b), a clematis vine seems to be wafting in spring breezes, its blossoms caught as they sway out of the frame. Like Kōetsu, Shōkadō responded to the pictorial tensions established by the floral motifs as he wrote his poems, modifying and balancing compositional weight on the decorated sheets.

Shōkadō's calligraphy is somewhat more conservative than Kōetsu's, for it follows the sixteenth-

---

5. Although they are called the "three brushes of Kan'ei [1624–1644]" (*Kan'ei sanpitsu*), the era name more correctly would be Keichō (1596–1615), since Nobutada died in 1614 and Kōetsu's Keichō-period calligraphy is considered his best.
6. For a range of Shōkadō's calligraphy, see Shimizu and Rosenfield, *Masters of Japanese Calligraphy*, cat. 96–102.

century *kana* style practiced by the Shōren'in school of princely calligraphers, indicating that these poetry sheets are rather early in his development. Here, Shōkadō held his brush at an angle, writing energetically in rapid, ribbonlike strands of ink; soon, he would alter his writing under the influence of the more elegant, fluent *kana* calligraphy of the eleventh and twelfth centuries that Kōetsu had emulated in his Metropolitan *shikishi*.[6]

Like Koetsu, Shōkadō did not align the subjects of text and image: there is the same discontinuity of literary and visual allusion. The poem on the summer *Hollyhock* refers to a New Year ceremony, while the poem on the late-spring *Clematis* evokes the loneliness of autumn. Once again, seasonal layering adds depth and resonance to the whole. The auspicious intent of the New Year ceremony, in which young boys gather pine branches, is reinforced by the hollyhocks vigorously blossoming atop a stately stalk; the lonely plea for long-standing friendship is echoed in the instability of the fragile clematis. Both refer to the longevity of the pine: in the first, it supports the auspicious occasion; in the second, it contrasts with the sense of vulnerability and evanescence. The poems, found in different sources, are nonetheless by poets who belonged to the group of *Thirty-Six Immortal Poets*. Therefore, these two poetry sheets probably were part of a set of thirty-six, which may have been mounted on a pair of six-panel screens. Or they may have been mounted separately as hanging scrolls, as are these two, for hanging in the *tokonoma*, or focal alcove, of a tea room. The casual calligraphy, the relaxed understatement of the simple motifs, the impressionistic fusion of poetic and pictorial meaning accord well with the aesthetic of *chanoyu*, the tea ceremony.

The creation of ensembles from parts having different origins is a process often repeated in the arts of Japan, but it might best be explained in relation to the tea ceremony. A tea master carefully chooses the various objects he will use in the act of making and serving tea, as well as the painting or calligraphy that he will hang in the *tokonoma* to be shared in aesthetic contemplation by host and guest. Each tea ceremony requires a unique ensemble of tea utensils, and it is in their selection and combination that the tea master expresses, and conveys to his guests, his individual aesthetic. Both Kōetsu and Shōkadō were deeply involved in the tea ceremony; the art of allusive juxtaposition of fragments from varied contexts was one in which they were highly skilled. By combining allusions to visual and literary traditions connected with the courtly past, these men created a strikingly new impressionistic aesthetic, one that depends for its power on the fusion of its disparate fragments rather than on the logical integration of its parts.

In the 1620s, Shōkadō became closely associated with the greatest tea master of his age, Kobori Enshū (1579–1647).[7] In stressing simple yet elegant ornamentation, Enshū's tea aesthetic diverged from both the humble poverty of Sen no Rikyū (1522–1591) and the flamboyant materialism of Furuta Oribe (d. 1615). A scholar of classical literature, Enshū was drawn to the poetry of Fujiwara Teika, and to the poetic theories that underlie the *Shin kokinshū*. His respect for classical literature was a major factor in the creation of his own aesthetic of *kirei sabi*, or "refined rusticity." Enshū often hung poet portraits, such as the Burke Collection's *Portrait of Fujiwara Teika* (Fig. 8), for aesthetic contemplation during his tea ceremony. Other fragments of courtly taste were also found suitable to the tone

---

7. See Brown, "Shōkadō Shōjō as 'Tea Painter'," Itoh, "Kobori Enshū."
8. Shimizu and Rosenfield, *Masters of Japanese Calligraphy*, p. 256.

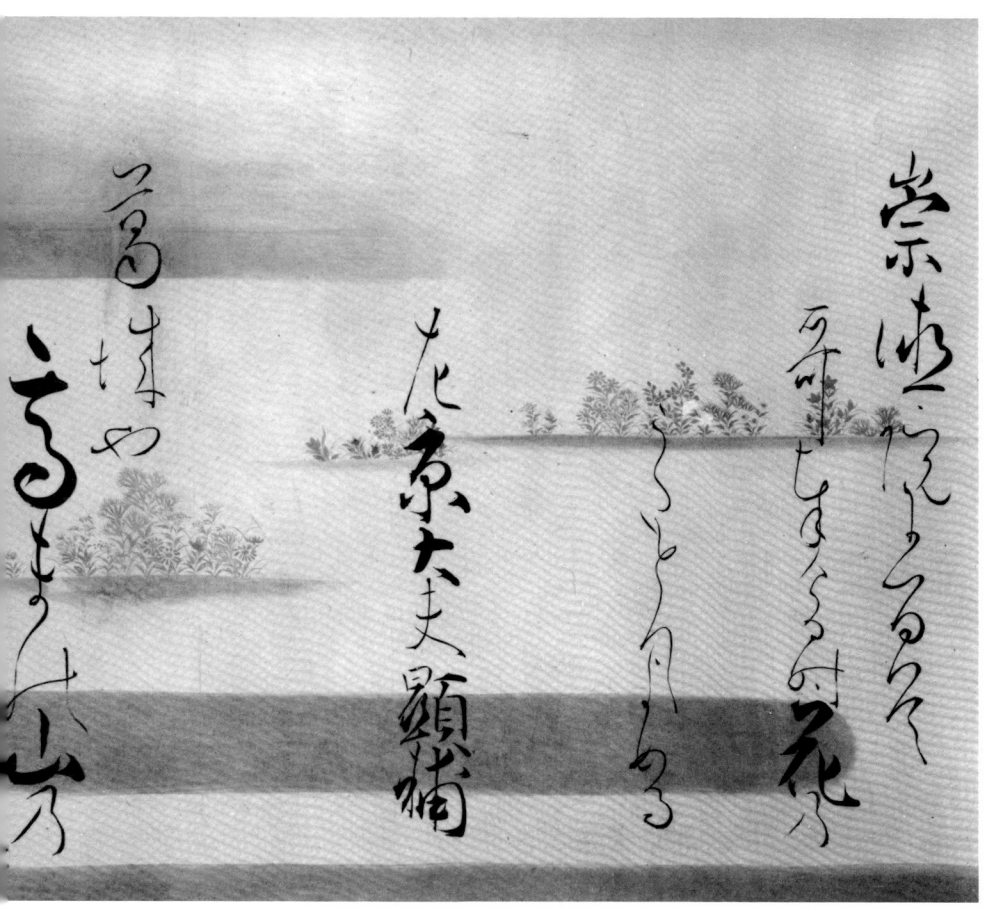

Fig. 53. Kojima Sōshin. *Senzaishū*, section (Cat. 41).

of subdued elegance desired in Enshū's tea room. He particularly admired Teika's calligraphy, reflected in the page of poetry from the Danziger Collection (Fig. 7) and, like others of his era, he emulated the irregularity of Teika's writing in his own calligraphy.

The multitalented courtier Karasumaru Mitsuhiro also showed his respect for the early-thirteenth-century poet by developing a calligraphic style based on the intense angularity of Teika's writing. In addition to being a courtier of high rank and a skillful diplomat, Mitsuhiro was a respected classical scholar and a keeper of the guarded secrets of the *Kokin denju* (see p. 18). It is fitting that he should follow Teika's style when he transcribed the *Tales of Ise* on the tinted pages of a lovely thread-bound book in the Harvard University Art Museums (Fig. 50). Mitsuhiro's rapidly moving, willfully turning, twisting brush links long strands of *kana* characters in active swings and swirls. The pronounced angularity of his brush movement and the frequent hooks that accent the beginning of strokes convey the impetuosity of a dynamic individual. Nevertheless, Mitsuhiro's flowerlike writing responds to the designs on the pastel pages of this volume, allowing the variety of painted motifs to add their graceful aura to the whole. The irises on the pages shown here are, of course, emblematic of the *Tales of Ise* (see p. 63).

Mitsuhiro excelled in poetry and painting as well as calligraphy. On several occasions, he inscribed his own poetry on paintings from Sōtatsu's studio, and he often created simple paintings with poetic inscriptions. Since he signed "Mitsuhiro" at the lower left of a page containing *Three Poems* in the Danziger Collection (Fig. 51), this sheet probably came from a book in which he wrote his own *waka*.[8] The dominant pattern behind the calligraphy in this case was created by the paper maker rather than a painter or printer. Long fibers dyed purple and blue were mixed with the paper pulp to create the relaxed, pendant forms that give it the

Fig. 54. Ogata Sōken. *Shin kokinshū Poetry Sheets.* Right: *Spring.* Left: *Autumn* (Cat. 42).

name of "cloud paper" (*kumogami*). With shifting light, however, we become aware of an ethereal landscape superimposed in fine lines of gold. A grove of palmetto, a flowering bush, and clusters of bamboo grass move in and out of representational space. A distant hill articulated by a line of cypress trees interacts with the cloud forms, which alternatively suggest mountains. Mitsuhiro's calligraphy seems suspended like flower garlands from the blue cloud-mountains, shifting from bold to fine to bold again, harmonizing with the bold curves of the cloud paper and the fine lines of the gold decoration.

Nobutada, Kōetsu, Shōkadō, and Mitsuhiro all were important participants in the process of creating an elegant aesthetic tone for their present by reusing the courtly past. However, it was Kōetsu who had the greatest impact on the artistic direction of both his own generation and those following. His powerful aesthetic is marked by its allusion to the literary classics, its layering of references to the courtly past, its craftsmanlike assertion of the formal qualities of materials, its collaborative creative process, and its fusion of text and image to the extent of their visual interchangeability.

During the first decades of the seventeenth century, Tawaraya Sōtatsu produced a number of decorated handscrolls on which Kōetsu wrote classical poetry—most frequently, *waka* from the early-thirteenth-century *Shin kokinshū*. These so-

---

9. Frequently published; see Minamoto Toyomune and Hashimoto Ayako, *Tawaraya Sōtatsu* (*Nihon bijutsu kaiga zenshū* 14) (Tokyo: Shūeisha, 1976), pl. 35.

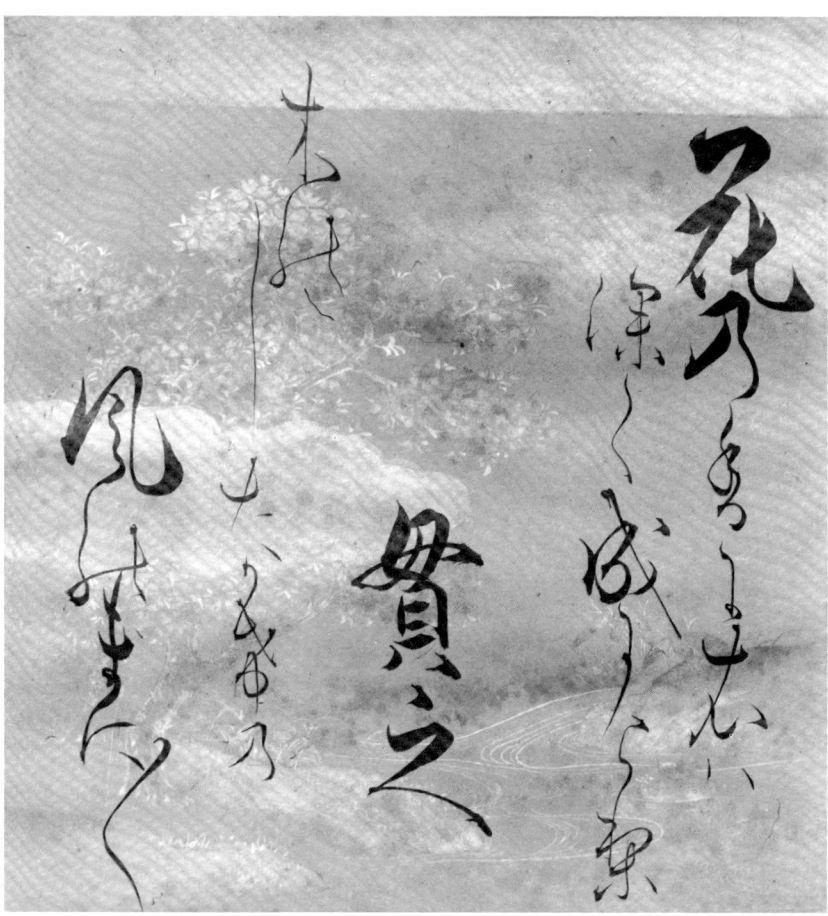

called poetry-painting scrolls are remarkable demonstrations of an extended creative process initiated by the artist, continued by the calligrapher, and influenced by both the nature of the materials used and the text of the poetry written. The Seattle Art Museum's *Deer Scroll*, created sometime around 1610, is representative of the group (Fig. 4; Cat. 39). Using gold and silver paint, Sōtatsu arranged deer singly, in twos and threes, and in herds—frolicking and fighting, resting and grazing, prancing and flirting. He suggested ground and sky with streaks of silver and gold paint, and left ample spaces for Kōetsu to write the poetry.

Deer are autumn motifs, and Kōetsu chose twenty-eight poems from the autumn section of the *Shin kokinshū* to write on this scroll. The alignment of season in text and image gives greater attention to the evolving mood and attitudes of the deer, which take on a slightly narrative quality as the scroll develops from right to left in time and space. In the section shown here from the Seattle scroll, a young buck bends to graze in a pose reminiscent of the deer Sōtatsu painted on one of the frontispieces of the *Heike nōgyō* that he restored in 1602.[9] Two more grazing deer are daringly truncated by the top of the scroll, causing the wave pattern of our gaze to extend beyond the frame and then be drawn back by their downward-pointing noses. Two prancing bucks bound gleefully toward the quietly grazing group, accompanied by three poems written in lines of varying length, height, boldness, and lightness.

Kōetsu's calligraphy is written rhythmically in counterpoint with the gold and silver deer. The painting is often calligraphic: the silver contours of the two leaping deer relate to the textures of the

Fig. 55. Kuze Shigeyuki. In no on'utaawase, ca. 1700, section (Cat. 43).

poems written before and beneath them. The calligraphy is often pictorial: the lines of poetry sway like autumn grasses beneath the two leaping deer, whose hind legs virtually kick the written lines behind them. In places, the mood of the poetry reinforces the mood of the painting: the first poem evokes a motionless image of the poet gazing at the full autumn moon; its fourth and fifth lines, "though the moon makes no choices among us," flank the quietly grazing young buck.

On the Deer Scroll, Kōetsu wielded his brush with swift decisiveness, delighting in the attenuation of trailing strokes, the three-dimensional turning of kana characters, and the stalwart boldness of emphatic lines. His robust style gradually changed during the next decade, becoming more lyrical. His scroll of Twelve Poems from the Shin kokinshū in the Burke Collection (Fig. 52) presents an elegant image of refined grace. On a ground of fine white silk, woodblock-printed motifs of the four seasons create golden textures while bits of gold leaf add mellow brilliance to hillocks and mists. This decoration progresses from the cherry blossoms of spring, shown here, through the grapevines and ivy of summer to the grasses of autumn and the pines of winter. Nevertheless, the twelve poems Kōetsu chose to write were taken from the autumn section of the twelfth-century Shin kokinshū. Rather than neutralizing the autumn mood of the poetry, the inevitable transitions of passing time add poignancy. A lonely longing for companionship sets the tone in the first poem of the scroll.

Tou hito mo arashifukisou aki wa kite
ko no ha ni uzumu yado no michishiba
—Shin kokinshū no. 515

There will be no more visitors: autumn has come with its storms,
and the grass in the path to my dwelling is buried in fallen leaves.
—Translation by Edward Kamens

Instead of the contrapuntal interaction of text and image that characterizes the Deer Scroll, these spiraling lines of calligraphy provide a light cadence from right to left along the undulating horizontal movement of the sparkling mists and hillocks. Instead of rhythmic vigor there is gentle buoyance and airy spaciousness.

---

10. Sōshin's writing reflects strong influence from the Chinese Southern Song calligrapher Zhang Ji-zhi (1186–1266).
11. See Stinchecum, Kosode, cat. 16–21.
12. See Komatsu, ed., Fukko wayō, pl. 9.

The elegance of Kōetsu's style of the 1620s and 1630s was the starting point for his followers during the remainder of the seventeenth century. In their poetry-painting scrolls and poetry sheets, however, Kōetsu's followers tended to replace Kōetsu's nuanced fusion of text and image with their own sense of fashionable elegance and pictorial lyricism. A good example is the scroll of *Poems from the Senzaishū* in the Spencer Collection of the New York Public Library, by Kojima Sōshin (1580–ca. 1655), a pupil of Kōetsu (Fig. 53). Along the edges of trailing gold clouds, clusters of dainty flowers blossom prettily in gold and pastel hues, with green garden rocks providing occasional accents. In vertical echoes of these miniature gardens, Sōshin used uniformly black ink to write thin lines of linked phonetic script punctuated with thick units of Chinese characters. Turning and twisting his wrist, he used the exposed tip of his brush to add decorative fillips at the opening and closing of strokes, pressing the heel of the brush to create jagged edges on the outer contours of curves and angles.[10] The structure of Sōshin's writing is broadly open in response to the ample spaces left between the delicate bands of the underpainting.

The spaciousness of Kojima Sōshin's calligraphy is as tasteful as the miniature gardens are ornamental, producing an effect comparable to that of fashionable kimono designs of the mid-seventeenth century.[11] The close interrelationship between the arts and crafts of Kyoto during the second half of the seventeenth century is embodied by Ogata Sōken, one of Sōshin's disciples in calligraphy. Sōken was the wealthy master of the Kariganeya, preeminent in the world of Kyoto fashion as the purveyor of fabrics to Tōfukumon'in (1606–1678), wife of Retired Emperor Gomizunoo. This cultivated townsman, father of the more famous Ogata Kōrin and Ogata Kenzan, produced poetry-painting scrolls extremely similar to the Spencer Collection's work by Sōshin.[12]

A pair of poetry sheets in the Burke Collection by Ogata Sōken, bearing poems from the *Shin kokinshū*, demonstrates his polished, if somewhat mannered, style (Fig. 54; Cat. 42). Compared with the magnified density of calligraphy and blossoms on Kōetsu's 1606 poetry sheet (Fig. 47) and the bold truncations of Shōkadō's *Hollyhocks* and *Clematis* (Fig. 49), Sōken's designs are pictorial and his calligraphy less personal. Over the scene of a cherry tree in flower by a mountain brook, Sōken wrote a spring poem by Ki no Tsurayuki referring to blossoms. He wrote the two characters of the

Past and Present 99

Fig. 56. Artist unknown. *Pampas Grass and Bush Clover*, ca. 1630s (Cat. 44).

Fig. 57. Follower of Tawaraya Sōsetsu. *Poppies*, ca. 1650–1675 (Cat. 45).

Past and Present   101

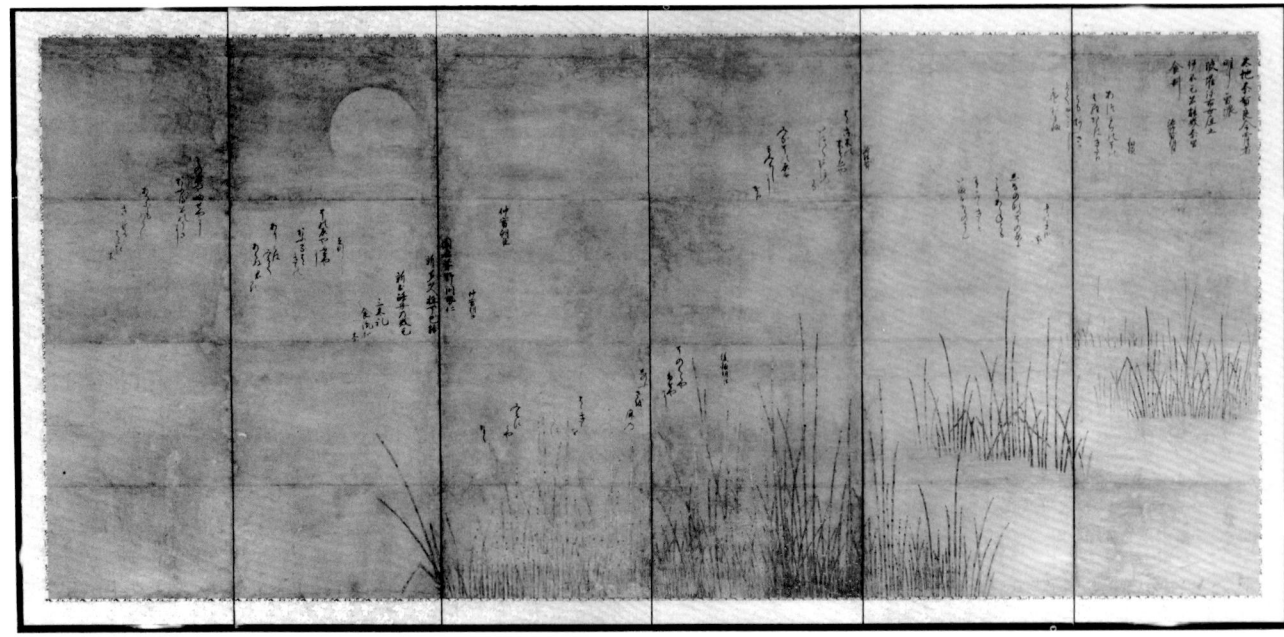

Fig. 58. Attributed to Konoe Nobuhiro. *Spring Azaleas and Autumn Rushes* (Cat. 46).

poet's name prominently in the middle of the sheet to emphasize the classical source. On the scene showing a stream swirling among autumn grasses and rocks, Sōken wrote an autumn poem by Fujiwara Ietaka, commenting on the waves of Kiyomi Strand. The first two lines on the right of this poetry sheet identify its classical source.

The literal, rather than allusive, quality of Sōken's *shikishi* is matched in a poetry-painting scroll written about 1700 by Kuze Shigeyuki, a scholar and government bureaucrat (Fig. 55; Cat. 43). The text is eminently classical: the poetry competition at the Retired Emperor Gotoba's court (*In no on'utaawase*) that Fujiwara Teika recorded in his diary, the *Meigetsuki*, on the fifteenth day of the eighth month of Kennin 1 (1201). Shown here are the pairs of competing poems for the twelfth, thirteenth, and fourteenth rounds, written with a brush moving swiftly over a spikey tangle of midsummer poppies. The dramatic spiraling of Shigeyuki's calligraphy holds its own against the strong gold-and-silver shading of the woodblock-printed flowers. The design is pictorial, with poppies growing from the base line of the scroll and remaining, for the most part, within the frame. Shigeyuki responded sensitively to the force of the flowers, rhythmically placing his bold accents and twisting lines to create a bold, linear texture over the floral motifs.

The interaction of past and present in word and image is conspicuous in large folding screens of the seventeenth century as well as in small scrolls and poetry sheets. Explicitly and implicitly, artists of large-scale works evoked classical literature to create layered allusions to the aesthetic past. *Pampas Grass and Bush Clover*, a pair of six-panel screens from the Metropolitan Museum of Art (Fig. 56; Cat. 44), is filled with the poignancy of autumn poetry by virtue of the rhythmic repetition of its two graceful motifs. From the oldest Japanese poetry collected in the eighth century *Man'yōshū* through the much admired *waka* in the early-thirteenth-century *Shin kokinshū* to the 1630s, when these screens probably were painted, pampas grass (*susuki*) and bush clover (*hagi*) appear again and again to enhance the melancholy of autumn. From at least the twelfth century on, gardens with dew-studded autumn grasses appeared in illustrations for romantic fiction, such as the *Tale of Genji* or the *Tales of Ise*, their presence intended to intensify the bittersweet emotions of love and longing.

Nor was the literary allusion of these autumn grasses diminished by the fact that they had been favorite motifs in crafts from very early times and continued to decorate functional objects. A design of bush clover on a Mino ware plate from the Seattle Art Museum (Fig. 62; Cat. 49), for example,

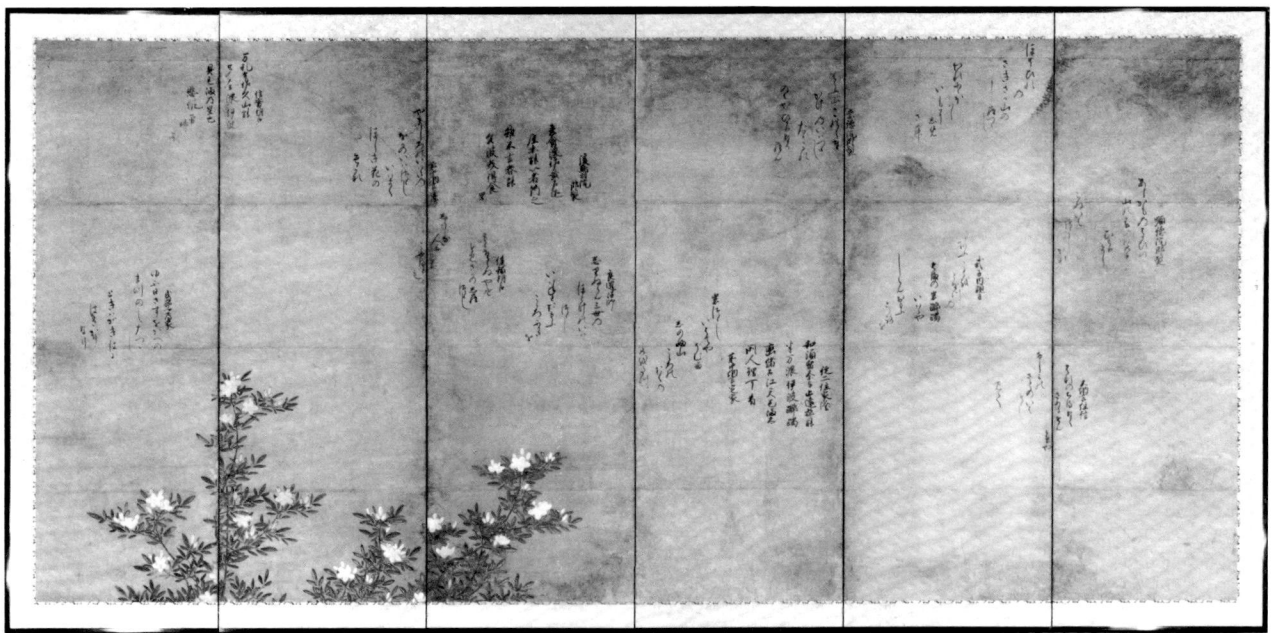

adds a sense of gentle tradition to an object used for the meal preceding the tea ceremony. When accompanied by a moon, as in the three-tiered lacquer box from the Danziger Collection (Fig. 45; Cat. 33), autumn grasses carry a further allusion to the Musashi Plain, a famous place repeatedly immortalized in *waka* and particularly associated with episode 12 in the *Tales of Ise*. The splendid *Musashi Plain* screens from the Virginia Museum of Fine Arts (Fig. 43), like these of *Pampas Grass and Bush Clover*, hover on the boundary between art and craft, indicating the artificiality of the distinction between "expressive" art and "decorative" craft.

Like Kōetsu and Sōtatsu in their small-scale poetry-painting scrolls, the artists of the *Musashi Plain* and the *Pampas Grass and Bush Clover* screens were aware of, and respected, the formal qualities of their materials. They were also sensitive to the appeal of repeated, stylized motifs that adorned such functional traditional crafts as textiles, lacquer, and ceramics. They freely adopted vocabularies of motifs that adorned small, precious, highly crafted objects and magnified them to cover the large scale of folding screens, which are, after all, functional interior furnishings.

The artist of the *Pampas Grass and Bush Clover* screens simplified the *susuki* to thickets of tassled stalks rising above multiple slow curves of long, graceful leaves. In contrast to the linear grace of the pampas grass, he repeated the patterns of small oval leaves of *hagi* in groups of three, adorned with long clusters of reddish-purple flowers. Unfortunately, the heads of the *susuki* and the blossoms of the *hagi* have lost most of their heavy pigment, which would have added tactile richness to the surface of the painting. On the right screen, the clumps of grasses are scattered over an abstract surface of gold leaf, appearing, nonetheless, to grow on rolling hills that extend beyond the boundaries of the screen, and conveying a sense of natural spatial recession. They continue into the upper right quadrant of the left screen, but are separated by an avenue of gold leaf from the tops of two large clusters of *hagi* and overlapping thickets of *susuki* growing up from the lower left boundary and occupying the very front surface of the painting. The stylized interplay of these two delicate motifs does not obstruct the perception of their natural growth. So, although poetic motifs from small-scale crafts have been enlarged on the Metropolitan screens, they suffer neither loss of intimacy nor loss of literary allusion.

Unlike *Pampas Grass and Bush Clover*, the motif of the screens of *Poppies* in the Museum of Fine Arts, Boston (Fig. 57; Cat. 45), does not have a long

Fig. 59. Tosa Mitsuoki. *Flowering Cherry and Autumn Maple with Poem Slips*, 1654–1678 (Cat. 47).

Fig. 60. Artist unknown. *Flowering Cherry and Autumn Maple with Poem Slips*. (Cat. 48).

Past and Present 105

poetic tradition. Poppies appear, in fact, to have been introduced to Japan as part of the interest in the natural sciences that is noticeable as early as the 1630s. Study of medicinal herbs, in particular, led to the establishment of herbaria, with a consequent awareness of newly recognized and newly imported botanical species.[13] Poppies as a painting theme appear about the same time and garnered popularity as the century progressed. The Boston screens probably were painted in the third quarter of the century by a follower of Tawaraya Sōsetsu, Sōtatsu's heir, who became painter-in-residence to the Maeda daimyo in Kaga Province (Ishikawa Prefecture) in 1642.[14]

The composition of the Boston *Poppies* is dramatic and is based on the same design concept as the Metropolitan *Pampas Grass and Bush Clover.* On the right-hand screen, only the tops of a stand of poppies are visible growing from below the lower edge and continuing into the first two panels of the left-hand screen. After a small space, seven full stalks are seen in their entirety, completely and spaciously standing tall in the final four panels of the left screen. The painting of the poppies themselves reflects the growing interest in empirical understanding of plants in nature, and there is a naturalistic continuity of pictorial space; nevertheless, the basis for the striking compositional concept is closely related to designs of traditional crafts.[15]

The composition of the Boston *Poppies* would have been inconceivable, however, without the intervention of Sōtatsu and Kōetsu's poetry-painting scrolls earlier in the century.[16] In creating those collaborative works, Sōtatsu as decorator of the paper or silk left the design intentionally incomplete so that Kōetsu would have empty spaces to use for his calligraphy. Such a practice led to the willingness to accept a work of art in progress as a dynamic image with a past and a future. It clearly influenced Sōtatsu's large-scale works, in which he boldly experimented with unusual contrasts of form and space, as well as with the shifting point of view that is a feature of handscroll design. The *Poppies* are completely satisfying in their present dramatic form, yet it is easy to imagine their transformation if a calligrapher were to inscribe poetry on the expanse of gold space, writing his words to interact spatially and thematically with the flowers.

Although interaction of the written word and the painted image only underlies the visual concept of the Boston *Poppies*, it is manifest on the screens of *Spring Azaleas and Autumn Rushes* (Fig. 58; Cat. 46). Distant mountains and foreground blossoming azaleas provide the visual context for thirteen poems written directly on the paper of the right screen; rushes growing in a misty swamp on a night of the full moon set the scene for eight poems on the left screen. The screens have suffered somewhat from an early restoration that included the rewriting of some of the calligraphy. Nevertheless, the total composition preserves the literary intent of the first half of the seventeenth century, and the calligraphy—some of it quite fresh and exciting—represents one of the major calligraphic traditions of the early Edo period, that which followed the brusque manner of the great Keichō-era calligrapher Konoe Nobutada (1565–1614) and is known, after his posthumous Buddhist name, as the Sanmyaku'in school.

Use of calligraphy as a meaningful decorative motif in combination with craftsmanlike design motifs for interior decoration has a long history in Japan, particularly in the format of decorated folding screens mounted with inscribed poetry sheets or poem slips. Records indicate that at least one calligrapher of the thirteenth century wrote directly on the surface of screens, but visible evidence is not apparent until the end of the sixteenth century, when Konoe Nobutada wrote his assertive, large-scale *kana* calligraphy on screens decorated with such designs as morning-glory vines or mountain ranges.[17] The decoration on the Salmon screens (Fig. 58) is more pictorial than the works of Nobutada and his immediate followers, presenting a unified landscape in minimal motifs. The calligraphy has been attributed to Nobutada's son, Konoe Nobuhiro (1599–1649), and reflects the Sanmyaku'in writing style near the middle of the century.[18]

The poetry and the painting complement each other. On the right-hand screen, all thirteen poems

---

13. See Guth, "Varied Trees," pp. 56–59.
14. See Shimazaki, "Kanazawa chihō ni okeru Sōtatsu-ha—Sōsetsu to Sōsetsu ni tsuite" (The Sōtatsu school in Kanazawa—concerning the two Sōsetsu), in Yamane, ed., *Sōtatsu-ha* 2, pp. 46–47.
15. Nishimoto Shūko, in fact, compares the composition to *susomoyō*, the designs bordering the hems of kimonos that became fashionable in the nineteenth century as a result of sumptuary laws; in Yamane, ed., *Rinpa*, commentary for pls. 42–43 on p. 130.
16. Guth, "Varied Trees," p. 54.
17. See Tamamushi, *Bijutsushi* 117, pp. 58–60.
18. See Komatsu, *Fukko wayō*, pls. 1–3, and Komatsu, *Nihon shoryū zenshi*, vol. 2, nos. 995, 997–1002, for Nobuhiro's writing.

Fig. 61. Black lacquer ewer with silver design of *Wisteria* (Cat. 50).

Fig. 62. Mino ware plate, Nezumi Shino type, with decoration of *Autumn Grasses* (Cat. 49).

Past and Present 107

mention azaleas, which can be seen blooming in the lower part of the three left panels. All of these poems were selected from the *Fubokushō*, an early-fourteenth-century poetry anthology, and over half were composed by poets of Retired Emperor Gotoba's circle, including Fujiwara Teika and Gotoba himself. On the left-hand screen, both the sources and the allusions of the eight poems are more varied. Five of the six sources are poetic anthologies, including the *Shin kokinshū* and the *Fubokushō*, but the sixth poem comes from the second chapter of the *Tale of Genji*, "Hahakigi." All eight of the poems refer either to *hahakigi*, the kind of autumn rush pictured, or to Sonohara, a place in Shinano Province (on the modern border between Gifu and Nagano Prefectures) that was famous for these reeds. The poetic allusion, therefore, includes a *meisho*, or famous place, so the painting could be considered *meisho-e*.

The arrangement of the poems in lines of varying length and height conveys a sense of light lyricism that adds to the evocative mood of the spacious compositions. Five poems have been written in *Man'yōgana*, using Chinese characters primarily for their sound rather than their meaning, and three of those (on panels R3, R4, and L1) create the solid effect that blocks of Chinese poetry often have, adding their heavy weight to the otherwise buoyant arrangement of the poems. Two others (on panels R5–R6 and L4–L5) are written in the same "scattered writing" manner used for the poems in Japanese phonetic script. The poetry seems to drift in and out of the vaporous landscape, creating a quiet mood of lyrical contemplation.

In contrast to the lyricism of the Salmon screens, the screens of *Flowering Cherry and Autumn Maple with Poem Slips* from the Chicago Art Institute are narrative in expression (Fig. 59; Cat. 47). Dating from the third quarter of the seventeenth century, they were painted by Tosa Mitsuoki (1617–1691), director of the Imperial Court Painting Bureau, for Tōfukumon'in, the wife of Retired Emperor Gomizunoo. The screens might be seen as a record of spring and autumn outings that the empress had taken with members of the imperial court. While eating, drinking, and enjoying the beauties of the season, those assembled would write poems on poem slips, celebrating the blossoming cherry or the red-leafed maple. Before leaving, they would tie their poems to the branches of the admired trees. Mitsuoki's lucidly composed screens show the sites of these entertainments suffused with golden mists just after the party has left, suggesting a haze of enjoyable memories. The poem slips are meticulously painted to indicate the richness of decorated paper, and the calligraphy of each poem is so distinct that, just a few decades after the screens were painted, a connoisseur felt confident in naming the calligrapher of each poem.

A second pair of screens on the same theme in the Danziger Collection is similar in style but radically different in composition and emotional expression (Fig. 60). While Mitsuoki's trees stand in dignified silhouette against the golden haze, these are enmeshed within a lush profusion of succulent white blossoms and burnished red leaves. The entangled poem slips reveal less of their poetry, and the decorated curtains stretched beside each tree suggest a more private party. Perhaps the sensuous surface and hidden depths of these scenes connote lovers on an outing, writing of their affection in the beloved words of court poets. By the second half of the seventeenth century, phrases from court poetry had become so well known to literate audiences that only a few ideograms visible on a twisting poem slip could quickly be identified and their refined context recalled. The words and images of the imperial court, once so jealously guarded by cultivated aristocrats, had become essential to the stylish elegance of the well-bred Kyoto townsman. The aesthetic past had become part of the continuing present.

Catalogue

Abbreviated titles of sources cited in this catalogue are listed with complete information in the Bibliography. Unless otherwise indicated, all translations of poems are by Edward Kamens. In the case of works published in several sources, two or three have been chosen on the basis of better quality of reproduction and ease of access to the source.

The Past in the Present: Fujiwara Teika and the Traditions of Japanese Poetry

Cat. 1 (Fig. 7).

Attributed to Fujiwara Teika (1162–1241). *Commentary on Poems* (probably from a poetry competition [*uta-awase*]). Hanging scroll, ink on paper, 23.5 x 18.0 cm. Peggy and Richard M. Danziger.

Unpublished.

Cat. 2 (Fig. 6).

Attributed to Emperor Goyōzei (1571–1617). *Teika Poem Written on Poem Slip*. Ink on poem slip (*tanzaku*) decorated in silver and gold paint, mounted as hanging scroll, 36.0 x 5.3 cm. Peggy and Richard M. Danziger.

Published: Shimizu and Rosenfield, *Masters of Japanese Calligraphy*, no. 81, p. 209.

The poem is *Shoku kokinshū*, no. 1790, originally composed as one of three poems on the topic "expressing one's feelings" (*jukkai*) at a poetry competition held in 1206:

> Omoioku tsuyu no yosuga no shinobugusa
> kimi o zo tanomu mi wa kienu to mo

> The delicate fern covered with dew
> I entrust to you, my lord, should I myself perish.

The "delicate fern" (*yosuga no shinobugusa*) is apparently a child whose future care is entrusted to another by a parent contemplating his own demise. The image of falling dew (*oku tsuyu*) and its eventual evaporation is linked to the parent's "lingering care" as he anticipates his own physical death (*mi wa kienu*), and the name of the *shinobugusa* itself suggests devotion and longing.

Cat. 3 (Fig. 8).

Artist unknown. *Portrait of Fujiwara Teika*, from the *Jidai fudō utaawase emaki*, ca. 1300. Fragment of a handscroll mounted as hanging scroll, ink and light color on paper, 37.5 x 28.7 cm. The Mary and Jackson Burke Collection.

Published: Mori, *Kobijutsu* 8, fig. 8; Murase, *Japanese Art*, no. 20, pp. 69-70.

The poem by Teika is *Shin kokinshū*, no. 487:

> Hitori nuru yamadori no o no shidario ni
> shimo okimayou toko no tsukikage

> What looks like frost on the long drooping tail of the solitary
> sleeping pheasant is actually moonlight falling upon his bed.

Cat. 4 (Fig. 9; color detail, Fig. 5).

School of Tawaraya Sōtatsu (fl. 1600–1640). *Sano Crossing* (*Sano no watari*). Single-panel screen (originally a hanging scroll), in color and gold leaf on paper, 126.0 x 121.3 cm. The Cleveland Museum of Art, John L. Severance Fund, 49.554.

Published: Lee, *Japanese Decorative Style*, no. 66, pp. 67–68; Yamane, *Rinpa*, pl. 50, pp. 133–34.

The image pictorializes Teika's poem, *Shin kokinshū*, no. 671:

> Koma tomete sode uchiharau kage mo nashi
> Sano no watari no yuki no yūgure

> There is no shelter in which to rest my horse or brush the snow from my sleeves
> at Sano Crossing on this snowy night.

Re-Presenting Teika's Flowers and Birds

Cat. 5 (Fig. 15; detail, Fig. 17).

Tosa Mitsunari (1646–1710). *Teika's Poems on Flowers and Birds of the Twelve Months*, ca. 1688–1710. Pair of six-panel screens, ink and color on paper, each screen 170.0 x 375.0 cm. Tiger Collection.

Signature on first and twelfth panels: "Tosa no kami, Jugoi-no-ge [Junior Fifth Rank Lower], Fujiwara Mitsunari hitsu"

Square relief seal: *Tosa Mitsunari*

Published: Takeno, *Museum* 414, pl. 6, pp. 12–13.

Cat. 6 (Fig. 16; detail, Fig. 2 and Fig. 18; color detail, Fig. 10).

Yamamoto Soken (fl.1683–d.1706). *Teika's Poems on Flowers and Birds of the Twelve Months*, ca. 1690–1692. Pair of six-panel screens with paintings in color on silk attached to each of the twelve panels: each painted panel is 105.0 x 50.0 cm. Mounted above each painting are two decorated *shikishi* with two Teika poems written by twelve courtiers: each pair of *shikishi* is 25.0 x 62.0 cm; each folding screen is 168.0 x 364.0 cm. The Director's Discretionary Fund, Archer M. Huntington, 1897h, Charles Stetson, B.A. 1900 and Wilson P. Foss, Jr., Funds, Yale University Art Gallery, 1986.5.1.1,.2.

Signature: "Hokkyō Soken" on panels 1, 6, 7, and 12

Square relief seal: *Soken* on all panels

Rectangular intaglio seal: *Hokkyō* impressed above the *Soken* seal on panels 2 through 5 and 8 through 11.

Unpublished.

Reference: Takeno, *Museum* 414: 7.

The calligrapher's names and titles, beginning with the first-month poems on the far right of the right-hand screen, are as follows:

1. Takatsukasa Kanehiro, Minister of the Left (1648–1725)
2. Koga Michinari, Major Counselor (1659–1719)
3. Daigo Fuyumoto, Major Counselor (d. 1697)
4. Imadegawa Koresue, Former Major Counselor (1659–1709)
5. Kazan'in Mochishige, Middle Counselor
6. Nakanoin Michini, Counselor and Guards Captain (fl. 1690)
7. Arisugawa Yukihito, Imperial Prince (1655–1699)
8. Kujō Sukezane, General of the Left (or Right?) (1668–1729)
9. Shimizudani Sanenari, Major Counselor (fl. 1672)
10. Jimyōin Mototoki, Former Middle Counselor (1634–1704)
11. Niwata Shigeeda, Former Middle Counselor (1650–1725)
12. Asukai Masatoyo, Third Rank (d. 1712)

If the court titles recorded with the names of these calligraphers are those they held at the time they copied the poems, the project was probably carried out no earlier than the third year of the Genroku period (1690) and no later than the fifth year of Genroku (1692). Takatsukasa Kanehiro, the highest officeholder of the group, takes pride of place as the calligrapher for the first-month poems; he eventually held the post of regent. Many of these men's families had histories of particularly strong devotion to the practice and patronage of the arts, especially poetry, calligraphy, and painting. Imadegawa Koresue was also a devotee of ancient musical instruments, especially the *biwa*; according to one story, his antiquarian fervor drove him to great lengths to acquire a *biwa* once owned by Emperor Daigo (885–930). Nakanoin Michini's father is said to have studied with the great painter Tosa Mitsuoki, while Kujō Sukezane is said to have painted "Sarasvatī's Fifteen Attendants" for Jōzen-ji, a Kyoto monastery. Three of these calligraphers—Kanehiro, Sukezane, and Shimizudani Sanenari—are also among the eight who joined with Soken to produce another calligraphic-and-pictorial project, a version of the "Eight Views of Ōmi Province" (*Ōmi hakkei*) in the Beinecke Rare Book Library at Yale University.

Cat. 7 (Fig. 19).

Artist unknown. *Shigi no hagaki*. Wood-block printed book containing twelve illustrations of poems of the twelve months selected from the *Hatakeyama Shōsakutei shiika*. Published in 1691 by Yoshida Saburōbei and Itō Heihachi, ink on paper, 22.5 x 16.5 cm. The Art Institute of Chicago, Martin A. Ryerson Collection.

Published: Nishimoto, *Kokka* 1043: 21; Kobayashi and Murashige, *Shōsha sōshokubi*, appendix (p. 175).

Reference: Toda, *Descriptive Catalogue*, p. 87.

Cat. 8 (Fig. 21).

Ogata Kenzan (1663–1743). *Teika's Poems on Flowers and Birds of the Twelve Months*, early-seventeenth century. Twelve square pottery plates, each 17.9 x 20.0 x 2.3 cm. Los Angeles County Museum of Art, Japanese Business Association and the Far Eastern Art Council, M.84.84.1–.12.

Signed: "Kenzan Tōin Shinseishō" (on reverse of twelfth plate)

Seal: *Shōko*

Published: Yamane, ed. *Kōrin-ha* 2, pl. 102 and pp. 117–20.

Cat. 9 (Fig. 22).

Kano Tan'yū (1602–1674). *Teika's Poems on Flowers and Birds of the Twelve Months*, 1672. Six-panel screen, ink and colors on silk, 158.1 x 368.3 cm. Mr. and Mrs. Leighton R. Longhi.

Signature: "Kunaikyō Hōin Tan'yū, *gyonen* 71 *sai hitsu* [painted at age 71]"

Square intaglio seal: *Seimei [Hōin]*

Gourd-shaped relief seal: *Hippō*

Unpublished.

Cat. 10 (Fig. 20).

Ogata Kenzan (1663–1743). *Teika's Poems on Flowers and Birds of the Twelve Months: The Fourth Month and The Sixth Month*, 1743. Two hanging scrolls in ink and color on paper; The Metropolitan Museum of Art, New York. The Harry G. C. Packard Collection of Asian Art, Gift of Harry G. C. Packard and Purchase, Fletcher, Rogers, Harris Brisbane Dick and Louis V. Bell Funds, Joseph Pulitzer Bequest and The Annenberg Fund, Inc. Gift, 1975.

a. Fourth Month: 22.8 x 41.4 cm

b. Sixth Month: 23.2 x 41.6 cm

Rectangular relief seal: *Tōzen*

Published: Shimada, ed., *Zaigai hihō*, vol. 2, pls. 64–65; Yamane, ed., *Kōrin-ha* 2, pls. 4 and 5, figs. 44–46; Shimizu and Rosenfield, *Masters of Japanese Calligraphy*, no. 110, pp. 29, 264–65.

References: Nishimoto, *Kokka* 1043: 19–31; Kobayashi and Murashige, *Shōsha sōshokubi*, pls. 155–160 and appendix (pp. 180–81).

Cat. 11 (Fig. 24).

Hon'ami Kōetsu (1558–1637). *Cranes*. Black-lacquer writing box with lead and pewter inlays and gold lacquer decoration, lid 23.2 x 21.8 cm; box 21.3 x 19.8 cm, height 8.1 cm. Seattle Art Museum. Gift of Mrs. Donald E. Frederick, 50.67.

Published: Lee, *Tea Taste in Japanese Art*, no. 127 and nos. 149–50; *A Thousand Cranes*, no. 41.

Cat. 12 (Fig. 23).

Mino ware dish, Nezumi Shino type, ca. 1600, with gray glaze and design of *Geese in Flight* in white slip, 5.0 x 17.5 cm. Cleveland Museum of Art. Gift of Mrs. A. Dean Perry, 59.55.

Published: Lee, *Japanese Decorative Style*, no. 50.

Cat. 13 (Fig. 27).

Kakiemon porcelain headrest, ca. 1680, decorated with *Quail and Chrysanthemum* in overglaze enamels, 14.6 x 9.8 x 7.3 cm. Seattle Art Museum. Gift of Martha and Henry Isaacson, 76.100.

Published: *A Thousand Cranes*, no. 83.

Cat. 14 (Fig. 1).

Black lacquer sake bottles with gold design of *Bamboo and Snow*, Kōdai-ji style, late-sixteenth century, height 20.3 cm. Peggy and Richard M. Danziger.

Unpublished.

Cat. 15 (Fig. 26).

Nonomura Ninsei (fl. mid-seventeenth century). Incense container in the shape of a *Wisteria Seedpod*, ceramic with overglaze enamel decoration, 12.7 x 2.5 cm. Peggy and Richard M. Danziger.

Impressed seal: *Ninsei*

Unpublished.

Cat. 16 (Fig. 25).

Old Imari ware porcelain covered bowl, mid-seventeenth century, with overglazed enamel design of *Chrysanthemums*, height 9.6 cm, diameter 23.2 cm. Peggy and Richard M. Danziger.

Published: Takeshi Nagatake and Seizo Hayashiya. *Edo 3: Imari, Nabeshima. Sekai tōki zenshū 8* (Tokyo: Shogakukan, 1978), fig. 16 on p. 135.

Images of the *Tales of Ise*

Cat. 17 (Fig. 29).

Tales of Ise (Saga-bon), published by Suminokura Soan (1571–1632) in 1608, printed book in two volumes, each page 27.2 x 19.4 cm. MS 268, Spencer Collection, New York Public Library, Astor, Lenox and Tilden Foundations.

a. Flight along the Akuta River, episode 6, from vol. 1
b. The Ise Virgin's Visit, episode 69, from vol. 2

Published: Murase, *Tales of Japan*, no. 19, pp. 86–90.
Reference: Toda, *Descriptive Catalogue*, pp. 14–18.

Cat. 18 (Fig. 30).

Tales of Ise (Saga-bon), 1629, printed book in two volumes, each page 27.4 x 19.0 cm; MS 278, Spencer Collection, New York Public Library, Astor, Lenox and Tilden Foundations.

a. Yatsuhashi, episode 9, from vol. 1
b. The Ise Virgin's Visit, episode 69, from vol. 2

Unpublished.

Cat. 19 (Fig. 32).

Artist and calligrapher unknown. *Tales of Ise*: The Broken Wall, episode 5; Flight along the Akuta River, episode 6; and Returning Waves, episode 7; sixteenth century. Handscroll fragment mounted as a hanging scroll, ink and mica on paper, 33.0 x 134.5 cm; hanging scroll height 168 cm, width 152 cm. Bequest of the Hofer Collection of the Arts of Asia, The Harvard University Art Museums (Arthur M. Sackler Museum), 85.110.A.32.1971.

Published: Itō, *Ise monogatari e*, monochrome pl. 3.

Cat. 20 (Fig. 33).

Artist and calligrapher unknown. *Tales of Ise*, mid-sixteenth century. Three small handscrolls, ink, color, and gold on paper, height 14.6 cm; length of scroll 1 is 865.5 cm, scroll 2 is 962.4 cm, scroll 3 is 1061.0 cm. MS 46, Spencer Collection, New York Public Library, Astor, Lenox and Tilden Foundations.

a. The Broken Wall, episode 5, from scroll 1
b. Flight along Akuta River, episode 6, from scroll 1
c. Returning Waves, episode 7, from scroll 1
d. The Ise Virgin's Visit, episode 69, from scroll 2
e. Azusayumi, episode 24, from scroll 2 (mounted out of sequence)

Published: Itō, *Ise monogatari e*, monochrome pl. 6; Murase, *Tales of Japan*, no. 18, pp. 81–85, and color pl. 3.

Cat. 21 (Fig. 31).

Thirty-Six Immortal Poets. Portrait of Ariwara Narihira with poem from episode 4 of the *Tales of Ise*, published by Suminokura Soan (1571–1632), ca. 1610. Printed book, ink on paper, thread bound in paper cover, 34.5 x 25.0 cm. Bequest of the Hofer Collection of the Arts of Asia, The Harvard University Art Museums (Arthur M. Sackler Museum), 85.27.TA.136.1971.

Published: Rosenfield, Cranston, and Cranston, *The Courtly Tradition*, no. 55, pp. 169–71.

Cat. 22 (Fig. 34).

Artist unknown. *Tales of Ise*. Accordian-fold album of paintings and calligraphy on poem slips (*tanzaku*), ca. 1725–1730. Paintings in the Tosa style, calligraphy by members of the imperial court; ink, colors, and gold on paper; each poem slip 35.8 x 6.0 cm. Bequest of the Hofer Collection of the Arts of Asia, The Harvard University Art Museums (Arthur M. Sackler Museum), 85.326.TB.8.1971.

a. Yatsuhashi scene from episode 9
   Calligrapher: Ōgimachi Kimimichi (1653–1733)

b. Mt. Utsu scene from episode 9
Calligrapher: Rokujō Arifuji (1672–1729)

c. Mt. Fuji scene from episode 9
Calligrapher: Nishinotōin Tokinari (1645–1724)

d. Sumida River scene from episode 9
Calligrapher: Aburanokōji Takatsune (1682–1746)

Published: Rosenfield, Cranston, and Cranston, *The Courtly Tradition*, no. 77, pp. 232–34 (the Yatsuhashi poem slip).

Cat. 23 (Fig. 35).

Artist and calligrapher unknown. *Tales of Ise*, third quarter of seventeenth century. Set of three painted books, ink, color, and gold leaf on paper, each book 23.5 x 17.5 cm. Yale University, Beinecke Collection.

a. Sumida River scene of episode 9, from vol. 1

b. Former Mistress in Kawachi Province scene of episode 23, from vol. 2

c. Nunobiki Falls, episode 87, from vol. 3

Published: Fukuda, *Kokubungaku kenkyū shiryōkan ho*, pp. 1–5.

Cat. 24 (Fig. 36).

Artist and calligrapher unknown. *Tales of Ise*, early-seventeenth century. Set of four painted books; ink, color, gold, and mica on paper; each book 32.5 x 23.4 cm. MS 85, Spencer Collection, The New York Public Library, Astor, Lenox and Tilden Foundation.

a. Mt. Fuji, episode 9, from vol. 1

b. An Emperor's Visit to Sumiyoshi, episode 117, from vol. 4

c. The Ise Virgin's Visit, episode 69, from vol. 3

d. Writing on Water, episode 50, from vol. 2

Published: Sorimachi, *Catalogue of Japanese Illustrated Books and Manuscripts*; p. 37 is the Mt. Fuji scene in color.

Cat. 25 (Figs. 37-1 and 37-2).

Attributed to Tosa Ittoku (fl. early-seventeenth century). *Tales of Ise*. Four of twelve album leaves, ink, color, and gold on paper, each 24.5 x 19.5. Harvard University Art Museums. Gift of Yanagi Sōetsu to Langdon Warner, 1946; Gift of Langdon Warner to the Harvard University Art Museums; 1946.50.1–12.

a. The Broken Wall, episode 5 (1946.50.4)

b. Returning Waves, episode 7 (1946.50.8)

c. Azusayumi, episode 24 (1946.50.3)

d. The Ise Virgin's Visit, episode 69 (1946.50.5)

Unpublished.

Cat. 26 (Fig. 28 in color; detail, Fig. 41).

Tawaraya Sōtatsu (fl. 1600–1640). *Tales of Ise*. Mt. Utsu, episode 9. Album leaf mounted as a hanging scroll; ink, color, and gold on paper, 24.4 x 20.8 cm. The Mary and Jackson Burke Collection.

Calligraphy attributed to the courtier Takenouchi Toshiharu (1611–1647).

Published: Murase, *Apollo*, pl. 5, p. 101; Yamane, ed., *Sōtatsu 1*, pl. 1; Yamane, ed., *Rinpa*, pl. 1.

Cat. 27 (Fig. 38).

Tawaraya Sōtatsu (fl. 1600–1640). *Tales of Ise*. Visit to Sumiyoshi, episode 68. Album leaf, ink, color, and gold on paper, 24.5 x 21.0 cm. The Cleveland Museum of Art. Purchase, John L. Severance Fund, 51.298.

Calligrapher: Hino Sukekatsu (1577–1639). A recently discovered inscription on the back names the calligrapher as "Hino Saishō Dono," Councilor Hino, rendering invalid the earlier attribution of the calligraphy to Iwakura Tomooki (1601–1660). According to Yoshiaki Shimizu, Councilor Hino could be either Hino Sukekatsu or his son Mitsuyoshi (1591–1630), but since Sukekatsu signed another of his calligraphic works "Sangi" (Councilor), he probably was the calligrapher of this poetry sheet.

Published: Yamane, ed., *Rinpa*, pl. 4.

Cat. 28 (Fig. 39).

Tawaraya Sōtatsu (fl. 1600–1640). *Tales of Ise*. The Sacred Fence, episode 71. Album leaf mounted as a hanging scroll, ink, color, and gold on paper, 24.5 x 20.6 cm. Nelson-Atkins Museum of Art, Kansas City, Missouri. Gift of Mrs. George H. Bunting, Jr., 73.37.

Calligrapher: unidentified.

Published: Yamane, ed., *Sōtatsu 1*, pl. 54; Yamane, ed., *Rinpa*, pl. 2; Shimizu and Rosenfield, *Masters of Japanese Calligraphy*, no. 94 and color plate, p. 28.

Cat. 29 (Fig. 40)

Tawaraya Sōtatsu (fl. 1600–1640). *Tales of Ise*. Nunobiki Falls, episode 87. Album leaf mounted as a hanging scroll, ink, color, and gold on paper, 25.0 x 21.0 cm. Lent by The Minneapolis Institute of Arts, the John R. Van Derlip Fund, 66.40.

Published: Yamane, ed., *Sōtatsu 1*, pl. 60; Yamane, ed., *Rinpa*, pl. 3; Shimizu and Rosenfield, *Masters of Japanese Calligraphy*, no. 95.

Cat. 30 (Fig. 42).

Artist unknown. *Scenes from the Tales of Ise*, second half of seventeenth century. Pair of middle-sized six-panel screens, ink, color, and gold leaf on paper, each 95.2 x 244.7 cm. The Cleveland Museum of Art, John L. Severance Fund, 69.127 and 69.128.

a. Detail of Yatsuhashi scene from episode 9, on the right screen

b. Detail of the Well Curb scene from episode 23, on the right screen

Published: Kita, *The Bulletin of the Cleveland Museum of Art*, pp. 252–67.

Cat. 31 (Fig. 43).

Artist unknown. *Musashi Plain*, late-seventeenth century. Pair of six-panel screens, color and gold and silver foil on paper, 168.8 x 379.7 cm. Virginia Museum of Fine Arts, The Glasgow Fund, 1983.135.1/2.

Published: Otsuka, *Arts in Virginia* (1984), pp. 16–21; Shirahata Yoshi and Nakamura Tanio, *Kinsei byōbu-e shūsei* (Masterpieces of the folding screen in pre-modern Japan) (Kyoto: Kyoto Shoten, 1983), pl. 52.

Reference: Takeda, *Keibutsuga, shiki keibutsu*, nos. 28–29, 70–75.

Cat. 32 (Fig. 44).

Mino ware, Ki-Seto type, dining dishes (mukōzuke), set of five, late-sixteenth century. Overfired ash glaze with incised designs of Iris. Peggy and Richard M. Danziger. Unpublished.

Cat. 33 (Fig. 45).

Three-tiered box for food (jūbako) with motifs of Musashi Plain (autumn grasses and moon), seventeenth century. Black lacquer with mother-of-pearl inlay, gold and silver; height 19.2 cm, width 13.5 cm, 1ength 15.0 cm. Peggy and Richard M. Danziger.

Published: *Nihon no shitsugei, Makie IV* (Tokyo: Chūō Kōronsha, 1978), color pl. 62.

Past and Present, Text and Image

Cat. 34 (Fig. 47).

Calligraphy by Hon'ami Kōetsu (1558–1637) and underpainting attributed to Tawaraya Sōtatsu (fl. 1600–1640). *Autumn Poem on Cherry Blossoms*, dated 1606 (Keichō 11.11.11). Poetry sheet (shikishi) mounted as a hanging scroll, ink on gold and silver underpainting on paper, 20.1 x 17.8 cm. The Metropolitan Museum of Art, New York. The Harry G. C. Packard Collection of Asian Art, Gift of Harry G. C. Packard and Purchase, Fletcher, Rogers, Harris Brisbane Dick and Louis V. Bell Funds, Joseph Pulitzer Bequest and The Annenberg Fund, Inc. Gift, 1975.

Inscription: "Keichō jūichi-nen jūichi-gatsu jūichi-nichi"

Square intaglio seal: *Kōetsu*

Published: Yamane, ed., *Sōtatsu-ha 2*, no. 8, color pl. 15 and p. 70; Shimizu and Rosenfield, *Masters of Japanese Calligraphy*, no. 85.

References: Itō, *Yamato bunka* 45: 42–48.

Poem by Kamo no Chōmei (1155?–1216), *Shin kokinshū* no. 397:

> Nagamureba chiji ni mono omou aki ni mata
> wagami hitotsu no mine no matsukaze
>
> As I sit staring in this autumn with thousands of
>   sad thoughts,
> here, too, the pine wind from the mountain, for
>   myself alone.

Kōetsu's version differs from all standard versions of the *Shin kokinshū*, which have the word *tsuki* (moon) where Kōetsu wrote *aki* (autumn).

Cat. 35 (Fig. 48).

Fujiwara Sadanobu (1088–1156). *Poems from the Tsurayuki-shū*, vol. 2, *Ishiyama-gire*, ca. 1112. Unmounted page from a bound book, ink and silver on paper, 20.2 x 16.0 cm. The Mary and Jackson Burke Foundation.

Published: *A Selection of Japanese Art from The Mary and Jackson Burke Collection*, no. 70.

Other pages from the two albums that were separated from the Nishi Hongan-ji set and sold in 1929 are in various collections: see Fu, Lowry, and Yonemura, *From Concept to Context*, cat. 22, pp. 72–73; and *A Thousand Cranes*, cat. 25, pp. 114–16.

Cat. 36 (Fig. 49).

Shōkadō Shōjō (1584–1639). *Hollyhocks* and *Clematis*. Pair of poetry sheets mounted as hanging scrolls, calligraphy in ink on gold and silver underpainting on paper, each 20.1 x 17.6 cm. The Metropolitan Museum of Art, New York. Purchase Mrs. Jackson Burke Gift, 1979 (34a); Purchase, Gift of Mrs. Russell Sage, by exchange, 1979 (34b).

Published: Shimizu and Rosenfield, *Masters of Japanese Calligraphy*, no. 96.

a. The poem on the *Hollyhocks* is *Shūishū* no. 24:

> Ōnakatomi Yoshinobu Nagon
>
> Chitose made
> Kagireru matsu mo
> Kyō yori wa
> Kimi hikarete
> Yorozuyo ya hen
>
> [By] Minister Ōnakatomi Yoshinobu
>
> [You] pine trees, whose lives are limited
> To one thousand years,
> From this day forward will live in eternity
> Now that the august person has plucked you.

b. The poem on the *Clematis* is *Kokinshū* no. 909:

> Tare o kamo
> Shiru hito ni sen
> Takasago no
> Matsu no mukashi no
> Tomo nakanaka ni
>
> Fujiwara Okikaze
>
> Not even the pines
> Of Takasago
> Can be my long-standing companions.
> Who, then, will I make
> My true friend?
>
> Fujiwara no Okikaze
>
> (Translations from Shimizu and Rosenfield, p. 236)

Cat. 37 (Fig. 50).

Karasumaru Mitsuhiro (1579–1638). *Tales of Ise*, ca. 1630. Calligraphy manuscript in a thread-bound book, ink on tinted paper decorated with gold and silver underdrawings, 22.6 x 17.3 cm. The Hofer Collection of the Arts of Asia, The Harvard University Art Museums (Arthur M. Sackler Museum), 85.231.TA.66.1971.

Published: Rosenfield, Cranston, and Cranston, *The Courtly Tradition*, no. 76, pp. 230–31.

Cat. 38 (Fig. 51).

Karasumaru Mitsuhiro (1579–1638). *Three Poems*. Formerly a page of a bound book, remounted as a hanging scroll, ink on "cloud paper," with underpainting in gold, 16.8 x 15.5 cm. Peggy and Richard M. Danziger.

Signature: "Mitsuhiro"

Published: Komatsu, *Nihon shoryū zenshi*, vol. 2, fig. 1387, on p. 412; Shimizu and Rosenfield, *Masters of Japanese Calligraphy*, no. 106, p.256.

The poems are probably Mitsuhiro's own, written in a private notebook.

> *Kozue miru ono ga samazama shigeru ha ni*
> *kayou mo kuraki mori no shitamichi*
>
> Each leaf on the branches overhead grows so luxuriantly
> the forest path that makes its way below them is very dark.
>
> *Itsuwari mo waga mada shiranu maki no to ni*
> *matsu yo nagara no tsuki zo fukeyuku*
>
> Ignorant of deception, I pass this night by the cedar door,
> waiting while the moon moves onward.
>
> *Wakaruredo waga furusato no omokage ya*
> *tabine no yume ni mata kaeruran*
>
> Though I have left it, in the dreams I see in sleep on my journey
> the image of my home seems to return again and again.

Cat. 39 (Fig. 4).

Calligraphy of Hon'ami Kōetsu (1558–1637), painting by Tawaraya Sōtatsu (fl. 1600–1640). *Deer Scroll*. Section of handscroll, ink and gold and silver paint on paper, 34.0 x 939.9 cm. Seattle Art Museum. Gift of Mrs. Donald E. Frederick, 51.127.

Signature at the end: "Tokuyūsai Kōetsu" with monogram (*kaō*)

Round relief seal: I'nen

Published: Tanaka, ed., *Hon'ami Kōetsu*, pls. 88–103; Yamane, ed., *Sōtatsu-ha 2*, no. 20, pls. 70–71; Yamane, *Rinpa*, pls. 7–8; Shimizu and Rosenfield, *Masters of Japanese Calligraphy*, no. 87; *A Thousand Cranes*, no. 58, pp. 171–73.

Shown are *Shin kokinshū* autumn poems, nos. 384–86.

> Dai shirazu
> Horikawa no Udaijin
> *Hito yori mo kokoro no kagiri nagametsuru*
> *tsuki wa daretomo wakaji mono yue*
>
> Topic unknown
> Fujiwara Yorimune (993–1065)
> I more than anyone have stared at the moon until my heart could bear it no longer—
> though the moon makes no choices among us.
>
> Tachibana Tamenaka no Ason
> *Ayanakute kumoranu yoi o itou kana*
> *Shinobu no sato no aki no yo no tsuki*
>
> Tachibana Tamenaka (fl. 1082)
> How I abhor the cloudless night
> with its autumn moon shining on Shinobu village, my refuge.
>
> *Hōshōji no nyūdō*
> *saki no Kanpaku Daijō Daijin*
> *Kaze fukeba tamachiru hagi no shitatsuyu ni*
> *hakanaku yadoru nobe no tsuki kana*
>
> Fujiwara Tadamichi (1097–1164)
> With each gust of wind, as jewel-drops of dew scatter from the *hagi*
> the moonlight finds a moment's lodging.

Cat. 40 (Fig. 52; color detail on cover).

Calligraphy by Hon'ami Kōetsu (1558–1637); printed design by a follower of Sōtatsu. *Twelve Poems from "Shin kokinshū."* Handscroll in ink and gold on silk, 33.7 x 939.0 cm. The Mary and Jackson Burke Collection.

Dated signature: "Genna 2 [1616] Kōetsu"

Square relief seal: *Kōetsu* at the end of the scroll

Rectangular relief seal: *Kamishi Sōji* [Paper-maker Sōji] stamped across a seam at the end of the scroll

Published: Murase, *Japanese Art*, no. 50, pp. 170–72; *A Selection of Japanese Art from The Mary and Jackson Burke Collection*, no. 77.

Shown are *Shin kokinshū* autumn poems, nos. 515–16.

> *Tou hito mo arashifukisou aki wa kite*
> *ko no ha ni uzumu yado no michishiba*
>
> There will be no more visitors: autumn has come with its storms,
> and the grass in the path to my dwelling is buried in fallen leaves.
>
> *Iro kawaru tsuyu o ba sode ni okimayoi*
> *uragarete yuku nobe no aki kana*
>
> The dew that changes the colors of the leaves
> lights on my sleeves and mixes with my tears: it is field-withering autumn.

Cat. 41 (Fig. 53).

Kojima Sōshin (1580–ca.1655). *Senzaishū*. Handscroll with calligraphy in ink over underpainting in color and gold on paper, 29.4 x 766.4 cm. MS 84, Spencer Collection, New York Public Library, Astor, Lenox and Tilden Foundations.

Signature: "Shinkokuken Sōshin sho"

Oval intaglio seal: *Shōsai*

Square relief seal: *Sōshin*

Published: Murase, *Tales of Japan*, no. 17, pp. 78–80. References: Rosenfield, Cranston, and Cranston, *The Courtly Tradition*, no. 61, pp. 190–91; Kuboki, *Kojima Sōshin wakakan*, pp. 57–60; Komatsu, ed., *Fukko wayō*, pl. 9 (poetry scroll by Sōken that is very similar to Sōshin's Spencer Collection scroll), pls.11–13 (Sōshin's calligraphy); Fu, Lowry, and Yonemura, *From Concept to Context*, no. 30, pp. 90–91.

> *Sutoku'in ni hyakushū no uta tatematsurikeru toki,*
> *hana no uta tote yomeru.*

Sakyō no Taifu Akisuke

*Kazurakiya takama no yama no sakurabana
kumoi no yoso ni mite ya suginan*
— *Senzaishū* no. 56

Flower poem presented with a 100-poem
    sequence to Sutoku'in.
Sakyō no Taifu Akisuke [Fujiwara Akisuke, 1090–
    1155]

Cherry blossoms on Kazuraki's Takama peak:
who could be happy seeing them only through
    the clouds.

Fujiwara Mototoshi

*Haru o hete hana chiramashi ya
okuyama no kaze o sakura no kokoro to omowaba*
— *Senzaishū* no. 86

Fujiwara Mototoshi (?–1142 or 1143)

"Let us survive the spring and then scatter us!"
— so the cherry blossoms must think about the
    winds that blow in deep mountains.

Cat. 42 (Fig. 54).

Ogata Sōken (1621–1687). *Shin kokinshū Poetry Sheets*. Pair of hanging scrolls, gold paint and ink on paper, each 21.0 x 19.5 cm. The Mary and Jackson Burke Collection.
Unpublished.

References: Yamane, "Ogata Sōken," *Bijutsushi*, no. 51, pp. 91–96; Yamane, "Ogata Kōrin," *Acta Asiatica*, no. 15, pp. 69–86.

a. The poem on the *Spring* sheet is *Shin kokinshū* no. 111, by Ki no Tsurayuki (ca. 872–945), with the two characters of the poet's name written prominently in the middle of the sheet.

*Hana no ka ni
Koromo wa fukaku
Narinikeri*
    Tsurayuki
*Ko no shitakage no
Kaze no manimani*

With blossom-scent
The fragrance of these garments
Takes on new depth
    Tsurayuki
In every gust of wind that blows
Beneath the shadow of the trees.

b. The poem on the *Autumn* sheet is *Shin kokinshū* no. 969, by Fujiwara Ietaka (1158–1237).

*Hyakushu uta tatematsurishi toki
Tabi no uta
Fujiwara no Ietaka Ason

Chigiranedo
Hitoyo wa suginu
Kiyomigata*

*Nami ni wakaruru
Akatsuki no sora*

Travel poem
submitted with a 100-poem sequence.
Lord Fujiwara Ietaka (1158–1237)

Although no promise
Kept me here, the night has passed—
Kiyomi Strand
Where now the waves are left behind
By the brightening sky of dawn:
    (Translations by Edwin A. Cranston)

Cat. 43 (Fig. 55).

Kuze Shigeyuki (1660–1720). *In no on'utaawase* (Poetry competition at the court of Retired Emperor Gotoba in 1201 [Kennin 1.8.15]), ca. 1700. Handscroll with calligraphy in ink on paper printed with floral patterns and painted with gold and silver, height 14.8 cm. The Hofer Collection of the Arts of Asia, The Harvard University Art Museums (Arthur M. Sackler Museum), 85.270.TA.106.1971.

Published: Rosenfield, Cranston, and Cranston, *The Courtly Tradition*, no. 49, pp. 154–56.

Round 12, on the eremetic autumnal topic of "wind blowing through pines by moonlight" (*tsuki no mae ni matsukaze*), pairs poems by Kamo no Chōmei (1155?–1216) and Kojijū (Lady-in-Waiting). Chōmei's poem is *Shin kokinshū* no. 397, the same autumn poem chosen by Kōetsu for his 1606 poem sheet (Cat.34), but correctly written with *tsuki* rather than *aki*.

Round 13, on the topic of "pounding silk robes in the moonlight" (*tsuki no shita koromo o tsuku*), pairs poems by Kunaikyō (d.ca. 1204) and Saki no gon Sōjō (former high priest: Jien 1155–1225).

Round 14 continues the previous topic and pairs poems by Retired Emperor Gotoba (listed as an unidentified court woman) and Fujiwara Teika.

Cat. 44 (Fig. 56).

Artist unknown. *Pampas Grass and Bush Clover*, ca. 1630s. Pair of six-panel screens, color on gold leaf, each 154.0 x 350.6 cm. The Metropolitan Museum of Art, New York, Arthur Wiesenberger Foundation, gift Louis V. Bell Fund, Dorothy Graham Bennet Fund, Pfeiffer and Seymour Funds, 1972.

Published: Nakamura Tanio, "Susuki hagi zu byōbu" (Pampas grass and bush clover screens), *Kobijutsu* 37 (June 1972): 18–83; Kobayashi and Murashige, *Shōsha sōshokubi*, pl. 68 (color detail) and pp. 126–27.

Cat. 45 (Fig. 57).

Follower of Tawaraya Sōsetsu (fl.1639–1650). *Poppies*, ca. 1650–1675. Pair of six-panel screens, in color on gold-leafed paper, each 150.1 x 355.0 cm. Museum of Fine Arts, Boston, Gift of Mrs. Scott Fitz, 11.1272 and 11.1273.

Published: Yamane, ed., *Sōtatsu-ha 2*, no. 79, pls. 176–77; Yamane, *Rinpa*, pls.42–43.

References: Shimazaki, in Yamane, ed., *Sōtatsu-ha 2*, pp. 43–49; Guth, "Varied Trees."

Cat. 46 (Fig. 58; color detail, Fig. 3).

Attributed to Konoe Nobuhiro (1598–1649). *Spring Azaleas and Autumn Rushes*. Pair of six-panel screens, ink and color on paper with gold wash, 165.0 x 345.0 cm. The Salmon Collection.

Unpublished.

Spring Azaleas. Thirteen poems that mention azaleas (*tsutsuji*) from the *Fubokushō*, a late Kamakura, privately selected, very freely conceived *waka* collection compiled by Fujiwara (Katsumada) Nagakiyo, a poetic follower of Reizei Tamesuke (1263–1328); completed about 1310.

R1.	*Fubokushō* no. 2207; Retired Emperor Juntoku (1197–1242)
R1–R2	*Fubokushō* no. 2216; Minamoto Tsunenobu (1016–1097)
R2	*Fubokushō* no. 2299; Unknown
R2	*Fubokushō* no. 2210; Princess Shokushi (d. 1201)
R3	*Fubokushō* no. 2206; Retired Emperor Sutoku (1119–1164)
R3	*Fubokushō* no. 2211; Fujiwara Ietaka (1158–1237); written in Man'yōgana
R3	*Fubokushō* no. 2212; Fujiwara Teika (1162–1241)
R4	*Fubokushō* no. 2224; Ryōsen Hōshi
R4	*Fubokushō* no. 2222; Retired Emperor Gotoba (1180–1239); written in Man'yōgana
R4–R5	*Fubokushō* no. 2228; Minamoto Toshiyori (?1055–1129)
R5	*Fubokushō* no. 2231; Ōe Masafusa (1041–1111)
R5–R6	*Fubokushō* no. 2252; Fujiwara Nobuzane (1177–1265); written in Man'yōgana
R6	*Fubokushō* no. 2243; Fujiwara Tameie (1198–1275)

Autumn Rushes. Eight poems that refer to *hahakigi*, this kind of autumn rush, or to Sonohara, a place in Shinano Province (on the modern border of Gifu and Nagano Prefectures). All but one poem are from poetic anthologies; the exception is from the "Hahakigi" chapter of *The Tale of Genji*.

L1	*Shin kokinshū* no. 913: Fujiwara Suketaka (the author of the poem is mistakenly identified on the screen as Minamoto Morokata; written in Man'yōgana)
L1–L2	*Goshūishū* no. 942; Sagami (fl. ca. 1050)
L2	*Goshūishū* no. 1128; Taira no Masaie
L3	*Kin'yōshū* no. 260; Minamoto Yoshikata (d. after 1155)
L3–L4	*Fubokushō* no. 4642; Minamoto Toshiyori (?1055–1129)
L4–L5	*Horikawa hyakushu* no. 647; Nakazane (written in Man'yōgana)
L5	*Shin kokinshū* no. 997; Sakanoe Korenori
L6	*Genji monogatari*, chapter 2, "Hahakigi" (final section)

Cat. 47 (Fig. 59).

Tosa Mitsuoki (1617–1691). *Flowering Cherry and Autumn Maple with Poem Slips*, 1654–1678. Pair of six-panel screens, colors on silk, each 142.5 x 293.2 cm. The Art Institute of Chicago, Kate S. Buckingham Collection, 1977.156 and 1977.157.

Signature: "Tosa Sakon Shōgen Mitsuoki hitsu"

Square intaglio seal: *Mitsuoki no in*

Published: Narazaki Muneshige, "Tosa Mitsuoki hitsu ōka fūju zu byōbu" (Screens of cherry blossoms and maple trees by Tosa Mitsuoki), *Kokka* 789 (December 1957): 393–96; Takeda, *Shōheiga*, pls. 68–69.

Accompanying documents:

1. Document dated Genroku 11 (1698).12.1 written by Fujimoto Ryōin, identifies the calligraphers of the poem slips, naming twenty-five courtiers.

2. On the wrapper is written: "A letter of certification by Fujimoto Ryōin, saying these screens of blossoming cherry and autumn maple were painted by Tosa Mitsuoki and the poems were written by courtiers. Lady Tōfukumon'in [1607–1678, wife of Retired Emperor Gomizunoo] donated these screens, which are fitted with metal crests of the Tokugawa's three leaves of hollyhock [*mitsu-aoi*]."

3. On the cover of the certificate box are two lines of calligraphy: "Screens of cherry blossoms and maple leaves; list of writers of the poem slips."

4. Inside the box cover is a written account of the screens: "This splendid pair of screens was painted by Tosa Mitsuoki, was a possession of Tōfukumon'in, and was given to Chaya Shirōjirō. Now, in the second month of Meiji 9 [1876], the screens are in the possession of [deleted]. The *waka* on the poem slips were contributed by courtiers. Fujimoto Ryōin authenticated all of this. Ryōin was a pupil of the master Ryōsa, his first pseudonym was Koshitsu and his early name was Kasahara Kizan."

The poems on the right-hand screen and their poets, from right to left, with each calligrapher as identified by Fujimoto Ryōin in 1698, are:

R1	*Senzaishū* no. 610: Emperor Horikawa (1079–1107)
	Prince Sanjō Kintomi (1619–1677)
	Shūishū no. 44: Fujiwara Chikage (d. 929)
	Kujō Kaneharu, former Minister of the Left (1640–1677)
R2	*Gosenshū* no. 106: Fujiwara Atsutada (906–943)
	Aburanokōji Takasada, Major Counselor (1625–1699)
	[Poem ?]
	Jimyōin Mototoki (1634–1704)
	Goshūishū no. 95: Fujiwara Sanemasa (1018–1093)
	[Calligrapher ?]
	Shin chokusenshū no. 464: Fujiwara Yorimune (993–1065)
	Honored Monk Kōken of the Sanbō-in
R3	*Kin'yōshū* no. 35: Minamoto Masakane (1079–1143)
	Tonsured Prince Dōkō of the Shōkō-in (1611–1679)
	Goshūishū no. 126: Minamoto Michinari (d. 1019)
	Ōinomikado Norimitsu, Minister of the Right (1637–1704)
	Shoku gosenshū no. 89: Fujiwara Okikaze (ninth century)
	Sono Motofuku (1621–1699)
	Gyokuyōshū no. 175: Fujiwara Kanesue (1285–1339)
	Nakanoin Michimochi, Major Counselor (1630–1710)
R4	*Kin'yōshū* no. 62: Minamoto Toshiyori (Shunrai; 1055–1129)
	Tonsured Prince Sonshō of the Shōren-in (d.1694)
	Senzaishū no. 55: Fujiwara Kinmitsu (1130–1178)
	Asukai Masaaki, First Rank (1610–1679)
	Shoku senzaishū no. 131: Fujiwara Takanobu (1142–1205)
	Nakanoin Michimochi, Major Counselor (1630–1710)
	[Poem ?]
	Chigusa Ariyoshi, Major Counselor (1614–1687)
	Kokinshū no. 49: Ki no Tsurayuki (ca. 872–945)
	Tonsured Prince Dōkō of the Shōkō-in (1611–1679)
R5	*Shoku gosenshū* no. 605: Sosonji Yukiyoshi (1180–fl. 1249)
	Honored Monk Kōken of the Sanbō-in
	[Poem ?]
	Prince Saionji Saneharu (1618–1677)
	Shoku gosenshū no. 129: Retired Emperor Sutoku (1119–1164)
	Hamuro Yoritaka, Major Counselor (1643–1709)
R6	*Shoku kokinshū* no. 1875: Retired Emperor Sutoku (1119–1164)
	Gojō Tameyasu (1618–1677)

The poems on the left-hand screen and their poets, from right to left, with each calligrapher as identified by Fujimoto Ryōin in 1698, are:

L1 *Goshūishū* no. 343: Fujiwara Tsunehira (1005–1072)
    Karasumaru Sukeyoshi, Major Counselor (1621-1669)
L2 *Shin shoku kokinshū* no. 620: Tonsured Prince Shōson (1303–1370)
    Yanagihara Sukeyuki, Major Counselor (1619–1679)
    Shin shūishū no. 1665: Tonsured Prince Shinshō (Priest Genshō; latter half fourteenth century)
    Nakanoin Michimochi, Major Counselor (1630–1710)
    Shin senzaishū no. 580: Fujiwara Tamesuke (1263–1328)
    Ōinomikado Norimitsu (1637–1704)
    Kokinshū no. 264: Monk Egyō (latter half tenth century)
    Tonsured Prince Shinkei of the Ichijō-in
L3 *Shoku shin kokinshū* no. 343: Mikohidari Tameshige (1325–1385)
    Tonsured Prince Gyōjo (1639–1695)
    Senzaishū no. 357: Fujiwara Shigetsune (Monk Soi, d. 1094)
    Ōinomikado Norimitsu (1637–1704)
    Shin shoku kokinshū no. 585: Saishō no Tenji (late-thirteenth, early-fouteenth century; daughter of Fujiwara Masaari; 1241–1301)
    Tonsured Prince Shinkei, Chief Monk of the Ichijō-in
    [Poem ?]
    Hino Hirosuke (d. 1687)
L4 *Gosenshū* no. 381: Ariwara Motokata (late-ninth, early-tenth century)
    Tominokōji Yorinao (1612–1658)
    Shin senzaishū no. 551: Minamoto Shigeyuki (939?–1000)
    Sono Motokatsu, Middle Counselor (1662–1738)
    Shoku gosenshū no. 420: Fujiwara Genshi (The Biwa Empress; 994–1027)
    Chigusa Ariyoshi, Major Counselor (1614–1687)
    Fūgashū no. 1580: Monk Kenshun (1299–1357)
    Seikanji Hirosada (1661–1707)
    Shoku shūishū no. 1382: Hōin Ryōshu
    Yanagihara Sukeyuki, Major Counselor (1619–1679)
    Shin sensaishū no. 581: Yūgimon'in (1270–1307; Consort of Emperor Gouda; 1267–1324)
    Tokudaiji Kiminobu (1605–1684)
L5 *Shūishū* no. 199: Monk Eigyō (latter half tenth century)
    Karasumaru Sukeyoshi, Major Counselor (1621–1669)
    Senzaishū no. 353: Monk Kakuen (twelfth century)
    Tominokōji Yorinao (1612–1658)
    Gosenshū no. 390: Anonymous
    Tonsured Prince Jiin (d. 1699)
    Gosenshū no. 201: Minamoto Kanemitsu (d. 966)
    Prince Tokudaiji Kiminobu (1605–1684)
L6 *Shin chokusenshū* no. 344: Fujiwara Shunzei (1114–1204)
    Tonsured Prince Shinkei of the Ichijō-in
    Shin shūishū no. 715: Tominokōji Sanenori (1264–1349)
    Kujō Kaneharu, Minister of the Left (1640–1677)

Cat. 48 (Fig. 60; color detail, Fig. 46).

Artist unknown. *Flowering Cherry and Autumn Maple with Poem Slips*, second half seventeenth century. Pair of six-panel screens, gold leaf and colors on paper, each 175.0 x 372.0 cm. Peggy and Richard M. Danziger. Published: *The Collector's Eye: Japanese Art Lent by Friends of Japan Society Gallery* (New York: Japan Society, 1989), no. 17.

The poems on the right-hand screen and their poets, from right to left, are:

R1 Top
    Shin kokinshū no. 110: Yamabe Akahito (eighth century)
    Shin kokinshū no. 114: Fujiwara Shunzei (1114–1204)
    Shin kokinshū no. 118: Mother of Prince Yasusuke (mid- to late-eleventh century)
R1 Bottom
    Shin kokinshū no. 108: Ki no Tsurayuki (ca. 872–945)
R3 Top
    Shin kokinshū no. 107: Lady Ise (?)
R3 Bottom
    Shin kokinshū no. 123: Minamoto Moroyori (1070–1139)
    Shin kokinshū no. 117: Monk Egyō (latter half tenth century)
R4 Top
    Shin kokinshū no. 104: Yamabe Akahito (eighth century)
    Shin kokinshū no. 103: Provisional Major Counselor Nagaie (1005–1064)
    Shin kokinshū no. 109: Anonymous
R4 Bottom
    Shin kokinshū no. 131: Retired Emperor Sutoku (1119–1164)
    Shin kokinshū no. 133: Retired Emperor Gotoba (1180–1239)
    Shin kokinshū no. 102: Fujiwara Morosane (1042–1101)
R6 Bottom
    Shin kokinshū no. 99: Retired Emperor Gotoba (1180–1239)
    Shin kokinshū no. 100: Fujiwara Shunzei (1114–1204)

The poems on the left-hand screen and their poets, from right to left, are:

L1 Top
    Shūishū no. 195: Ōnakatomi Yoshinobu (921–991)
L3 Top
    Shūishū no. 210: Fujiwara Kintō (996–1041)
L3 Bottom
    Kokinshū no. 421: Monk Sosei (late-tenth century)
    Shūishū no. 200: Minamoto Nobumitsu
    Shūishū no. 190: Ōnakatomi Yoshinobu (921–991)
L4 Top
    Shūishū no. 197: Monk Kenshu
    Shūishū no. 199: Monk Egyō (latter half tenth century)
    Shūishū no. 208: Ki no Tsurayuki (ca. 872–945)
L4 Bottom
    Shūishū no. 189: Ōnakatomi Yoshinobu (921–991)
L5 Top
    Shūishū no. 196: Anonymous
    Shūishū no. 194: Anonymous
L5 Bottom
    Kokinshū no. 309: Monk Sosei (late-tenth century)
L6 Bottom
    Kokinshū no. 215: Anonymous
    Kokinshū no. 223: Anonymous
    Shūishū no. 193: Monk Egyō (latter half tenth century)

Cat. 49 (Fig. 62).

Mino ware plate, Nezumi Shino type, late sixteenth or early seventeenth century. Stoneware with transparent feldspathic glaze over iron rich slip and incised decoration of *Autumn Grasses*, 23.3 x 20.2 cm. Seattle Art Museum. Gift of Mrs. John C. Atwood, Jr. 51.205.

Published: *A Thousand Cranes*, no. 76, p. 205.

Cat. 50 (Fig. 61).

Ewer with design of *Wisteria* in silver on black lacquer; late sixteenth, or early seventeenth century, height 25.0 cm x width 23.0 cm. The Mary and Jackson Burke Foundation.

Japanese Historical Periods

Jōmon	2000–300 B.C.
Yayoi	300 B.C.–A.D. 200
Kofun (Tumulus)	200–552
Asuka (Suiko)	552–645
Hakuhō (Early Nara)	645–710
Tempyō (Late Nara)	710–794
Jōgan (Early Heian)	794–897
Fujiwara (Middle Heian)	897–1086
Insei (Late Heian)	1086–1185
Kamakura	1185–1333
Muromachi (Ashikaga)	1333–1573
Momoyama	1573–1615
Edo (Tokugawa)	1615–1868
Meiji	1868–1912
Taishō	1912–1926
Shōwa	1926–1989
Heisei	1989–

Map of Central Japan: Important Sites in *The Tales of Ise*

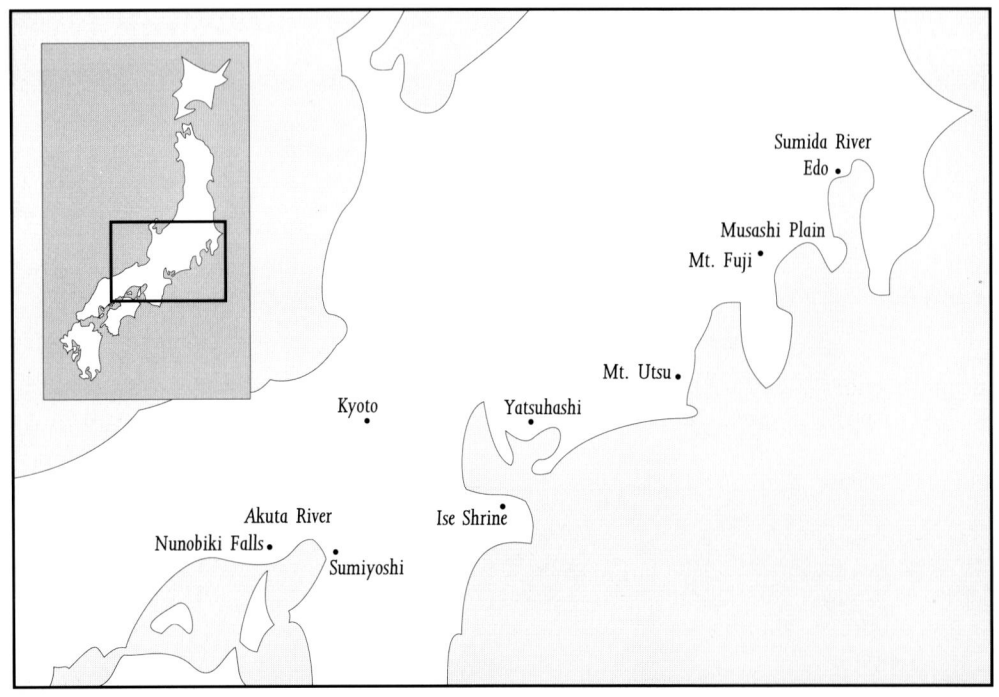

Selected Bibliography

Translations of Series Titles

Kachōga no sekai (The world of flower and bird painting)

Kanshō Nihon koten bungaku (An appreciation of Japanese classical literature)

Nihon bijutsu kaiga zenshū (Japanese painting series)

Nihon byōbu-e shūsei (Japanese screen paintings)

Nihon kagaku taikei (Japanese poetry)

Nihon koten bungaku taikei (Japanese classical literature)

Nihon meiseki sōkan (Outstanding Japanese calligraphy)

Nihon no sho (Japanese calligraphy)

Ōchō no kajin (Poets of the court age)

Rinpa kaiga zenshū (Rinpa painting)

Shodō geijutsu (The art of calligraphy)

Zaigai Nihon no shihō (Japanese treasures abroad)

Zusetsu Nihon koten bungaku (Japanese classical literature illustrated)

General

Adachi Keiko. "Muromachi jidai yamato-e byōbu jitsugetsu kachōzu ni tsuite" (Muromachi period *yamato-e* screens of flowers and birds with the sun and the moon). *Kokka* 1083 (October 1985): 13–32.

Brower, Robert H., and Earl Miner. *Fujiwara Teika's Superior Poems of Our Time: A Thirteenth-Century Poetic Treatise and Sequence.* Stanford: Stanford University Press, 1967.

―――. *Japanese Court Poetry.* Stanford: Stanford University Press, 1961.

Harootunian, H. D. *Things Seen and Unseen: Discourse and Ideology in Tokugawa Nativism.* Chicago and London: University of Chicago Press, 1988.

Higuchi Yoshimaro. *Gotoba'in.* (*Ōchō no kajin* 10). Tokyo: Shūeisha, 1985.

Kobayashi Tadashi and Murashige Yasushi. *Shōsha sōshokubi* (Elegant decorative beauty). (*Kachōga no sekai* 5). Tokyo: Gakken, 1981.

Lee, Sherman E. *Japanese Decorative Style.* Cleveland: Cleveland Museum of Art, 1961.

―――. *Tea Taste in Japanese Art.* Cleveland: Cleveland Museum of Art, 1963.

McCullough, Helen C. *Brocade by Night: "Kokin Wakashū" and the Court Style in Japanese Classical Poetry.* Stanford: Stanford University Press, 1985.

―――, trans. *Kokin Wakashū.* Stanford: Stanford University Press, 1985.

Miner, Earl, Hiroko Odagiri, and Robert E. Morrell. *The Princeton Companion to Classical Japanese Literature.* Princeton: Princeton University Press, 1985.

Mitchell, W. J. T. *Iconology: Image, Text, Ideology.* Chicago: University of Chicago Press, 1986.

Murase, Miyeko. *Japanese Art: Selections from the Mary and Jackson Burke Collection.* New York: The Metropolitan Museum of Art, 1975.

―――. *Tales of Japan: Scrolls and Prints from the New York Public Library.* New York: Oxford University Press, 1986.

Pollack, David. *The Fracture of Meaning: Japan's Synthesis of China from the Eighth through the Eighteenth Centuries.* Princeton: Princeton University Press, 1986.

Rosenfield, John M., Fumiko E. Cranston, and Edwin A. Cranston. *The Courtly Tradition in Japanese Art and Literature: Selections from the Hofer and Hyde Collections.* Cambridge, Mass.: Fogg Art Museum, Harvard University, 1973.

A Selection of Japanese Art from The Mary and Jackson Burke Collection. Tokyo: Tokyo National Museum, 1985.

Shimada Shūjirō, ed. *Zaigai hihō* (Treasures abroad). Vol. 2. Tokyo: Gakushū Kenkyūsha, 1969.

Shimizu, Yoshiaki, and John M. Rosenfield. *Masters of Japanese Calligraphy.* New York: The Asia House Galleries/Japan House Gallery, 1984.

Takeda Tsuneo. *Kano Tan'yū.* (*Nihon bijutsu kaiga zenshū* 5). Tokyo: Shūeisha, 1976.

A Thousand Cranes. Seattle: Seattle Art Museum, 1987.

Toda, Kenji. *Descriptive Catalogue of Japanese and Chinese Illustrated Books in the Ryerson Library of the Art Institute of Chicago.* Chicago: Donnelly and Sons, 1931.

Ueda, Makoto. *Literary and Art Theories in Japan.* Cleveland: The Press of Case Western Reserve University, 1967.

Yamane Yūzō. "Ogata Kōrin and the Art of the Genroku Era." *Acta Asiatica*, no. 15 (1968): 69–86.

―――. "Ogata Sōken hitsu 'Ise monogatari zu' byōbu ni tsuite" (Screens of "The Tales of Ise" by Ogata Sōken). *Bijutsushi* 51 (1962): 91–96.

―――, ed. *Kōrin-ha 2* (Kōrin school, 2). (*Rinpa kaiga zenshū* 4). Tokyo: Nihon Keizai Shinbunsha, 1979.

―――, ed. *Rinpa.* (*Zaigai Nihon no shihō* 5). Tokyo: Mainichi Shinbunsha, 1979.

―――, ed. *Sōtatsu-ha 1* (Sōtatsu school, 1). (*Rinpa kaiga zenshū* 1). Tokyo: Nihon Keizai Shinbunsha, 1977.

―――, ed. *Sōtatsu-ha 2* (Sōtatsu school, 2). (*Rinpa kaiga zenshū* 2). Tokyo: Nihon Keizai Shinbunsha, 1978.

The Past in the Present: Fujiwara Teika and the Traditions of Japanese Poetry

Higuchi Yoshimaro. *Gotoba'in.* (*Ōchō no kajin* 10). Tokyo: Shūeisha, 1985.

Imagawa Fumio, ed. *Kundoku Meigetsuki.* 6 vols. Tokyo: Kawade Shobō Shinsha, 1978.

Karasumaru Mitsuhiro. *Jiteiki.* See Sasaki Nobutsuna, ed. *Nihon kagaku taikei* (Japanese poetry), 6:142–208. Tokyo: Kazama Shobō, 1956.

Konparu Zenchiku. "Teika." See Yokomichi Mario and Omote Akira, eds. *Yōkyokushū* (Anthology of nō texts), 2:46–53. (*Nihon koten bungaku taikei* 41). Tokyo: Iwanami Shoten, 1963.

Kubota Jun. *Fujiwara Teika.* (*Ōchō no kajin* 9). Tokyo: Shūeisha, 1984.

_____, ed. *Yakuchū Fujiwara Teika zenkashū* (The complete poetry of Fujiwara Teika with commentary). 2 vols. Tokyo: Kawade Shobō Shinsha, 1985.

Mori Tōru. "Jidai fudō utaawase e" (Pictures of the poetry competition of poets of different periods). *Kobijutsu* 8 (March 1965): 25–74.

Shimazu Tadao. "Jiteiki o megutte." *Kokugo kokubun* 42, no. 6 (June 1973): 1–8.

Tsuchida Masao. *Hosokawa Yūsai no kenkyū.* Tokyo: Kasama Shoin, 1976.

Zeami Motokiyo. *Yūgaku shudō fūken.* See Nishio Minoru, ed. *Nōgakuron shū* (Treatises on nō), pp. 440–46. (*Nihon koten bungaku taikei* 65). Tokyo: Iwanami Shoten, 1961.

Re-Presenting Teika's *Flowers and Birds*

Bowring, Richard. *Murasaki Shikibu, Her Diary and Poetic Memoirs.* Princeton: Princeton University Press, 1982.

Kawahara, Masahiko. *The Ceramic Art of Ogata Kenzan.* Translated by Richard L. Wilson. Tokyo and San Francisco: Kodansha International, 1985.

Kenzan no kaiga (Kenzan's painting). Tokyo: Gotoh Bijutsukan, 1982.

Matsushita Takaaki. "Kenzan hitsu jūnikagetsu waka kachō zu ni tsuite" (Paintings of the Poems on Flowers and Birds of the Twelve Months by Kenzan). *Bijutsu kenkyū* 184 (January 1956): 194–200.

Nishimoto Shukō. "Ogata Kenzan hitsu 'Teika ei jūnikagetsu kachō zu' ni tsuite" (Ogata Kenzan's paintings of Teika's Flowers and Birds of the Twelve Months). *Kokka* 1043 (June 1981): 19–31.

_____. "Ogata Kōrin hitsu jūnikagetsu utai-e byōbu ni tsuite" (Paintings of poems of the twelve months by Ogata Kenzan). *Kokka* 1006 (May 1977): 7–26; and 1007 (June 1977): 19–26.

Takeno Megumi. "Kinsei ni okeru 'Teika ei tsukinami kachō uta-e' no tenkai" (The evolution of paintings of Teika's Poems on Flowers and Birds of the Twelve Months in the early-modern era). *Museum* 414 (September 1985): 4–17.

Tanomura Tadao. "Kōrin no shi Yamamoto Soken no gaseki" (The paintings of Kōrin's teacher Yamamoto Soken). *Kokka* 787 (October 1957): 311–20, and 788 (November 1957): 351–58.

_____. "Soken no Teika ei kachō waka-e" (Soken's paintings of Teika's flower and bird poems). *Kokka* 802 (January 1959): 6–10, and 803 (February 1959): 43–47.

Yoshida Yūji. "Kinsei Tosa-ha, Mitsunori kara Mitsuoki e" (The Tosa school in the early-modern age, from Mitsunori to Mitsuoki). *Kobijutsu* 71 (July 1984): 56–74.

Images of the *Tales of Ise*

Akiyama Tetsuo, ed. *Taketori monogatari, Ise monogatari.* (*Zusetsu Nihon no koten* 4). Tokyo: Shūeisha, 1978.

Fukuda Shūichi. "Ēru Daigaku Toshokan zō Nara ehon *Ise monogatari*" (The Nara picture-book of *The Tales of Ise* owned by the Yale University Library). *Kokubungaku kenkyū shiryōkan ho* (March 1981): 1–5.

Itō Masayoshi. "*Ise monogatari* to yōkyoku" (*The Tales of Ise* and nō texts). In Katagiri Yōichi, ed., *Ise monogatari, Yamato monogatari*, pp. 359–68. (*Kanshō, Nihon koten bungaku* 5). Tokyo: Kadokawa Shoten, 1975.

Itō Toshiko. "Den Sōtatsu hitsu *Ise monogatari* zu shikishi no shisho ni tsuite" (The texts on the *The Tales of Ise* poetry sheets attributed to Sōtatsu). *Yamato bunka* 59 (March 1974): 28–55.

_____. *Ise monogatari e* (Paintings of *The Tales of Ise*). Tokyo: Kadokawa Shoten, 1984.

Kita, Sandy. "An Illustration of the *Ise monogatari*: Matabei and the Two Worlds of Ukiyo." *The Bulletin of the Cleveland Museum of Art* (September 1984): 252–67.

McCullough, Helen Craig, trans. *Tales of Ise: Lyrical Episodes from Tenth-Century Japan.* Stanford: Stanford University Press, 1968.

Murase, Miyeko. "Themes from Three Romantic Narratives of the Heian Period." *Apollo* 276 (February 1985): 100–107.

Nakamachi Keiko. "Musashino zu no keifu" (The lineage of paintings of Musashi Plain). In Kobayashi Tadashi and Murashige Yasushi, *Shōsha sōshokubi* (Elegant decorative beauty), pp. 124–30. (*Kachōga no sekai* 5). Tokyo: Gakken, 1981.

Nara ehon kokusai kenkyū kaigi (International Research Conference on Nara ehon), ed. *Zaigai Nara ehon* (Nara picture books abroad). Tokyo: Kadokawa Shoten, 1981.

Otsuka, Ronald Y. "Musashi Plain: A Pair of Japanese Screens Depicting Autumn Grasses, the Moon, and Mt. Fuji." *Arts in Virginia* 25, no. 1 (1984): 16–21.

Sayre, Charles Franklin. "Illustrations of the *Ise monogatari*: Survival and Revival of Heian Court Culture." Ph.D. dissertation, Yale University, 1978.

Sorimachi, Shigeo. *Catalogue of Japanese Illustrated Books and Manuscripts in the Spencer Collection of the New York Public Library.* Revised and enlarged edition. Tokyo: The Kōbunsō, 1978.

Takeda Tsuneo, ed. *Keibutsuga: shiki keibutsu* (Scenic painting: Four seasons scenic painting). (*Nihon byōbu-e shūsei* 9). Tokyo: Kōdansha, 1977.

Yamane Yūzō. "Den Sōtatsu hitsu *Ise monogatari* zu senmen, byōbu shikishi" (Fans, folding screens, and poetry sheets of *The Tales of Ise* attributed to Sōtatsu). In *Sōtatsu-ha* 1 (Sōtatsu school 1), pp. 27–47. (*Rinpa kaiga zenshū* 1). Tokyo: Nihon Keizai Shinbunsha, 1977.

———. "Den Sōtatsu hitsu *Ise monogatari zu shikishi ni tsuite*" (*The Tales of Ise* poetry sheets attributed to Sōtatsu). *Yamato bunka* 59 (March 1974): 1–27.

Yashiro Yukio. "Sōtatsu hitsu *Ise monogatari jō ni tsuite*" (*The Tales of Ise Album* by Sōtatsu). *Bijutsu kenkyū* 98 (February 1940): 37–42.

Past and Present, Text and Image

Brown, Kendall H. "Shōkadō Shōjō as 'Tea Painter.' " *Chanoyu Quarterly*, no. 49 (1987): 7–40.

Fu, Shen, Glenn D. Lowry, and Ann Yonemura. *From Concept to Context: Approaches to Asian and Islamic Calligraphy*, no. 30, pp. 90–91. Washington, D.C.: Freer Gallery of Art, 1986.

Guth, Christine M. E. " 'Varied Trees': An I'nen Seal Screen in the Freer Gallery of Art." *Archives of Asian Art* 39 (1986): 48–61.

Itoh, Teiji. "Kobori Enshū." *Chanoyu Quarterly*, no. 44 (1985): 7–37.

Itō Toshiko. "Keichō jūichi-nen jūichi-gatsu jūichi-nichi no Kōetsu shikishi" (Kōetsu poetry sheets dated Keichō 11.11.11). *Yamato bunka* 45 (August 1966): 42–48.

Komatsu Shigemi. *Nihon shoryū zenshi*. 2 vols. Tokyo: Kōdansha, 1970.

———, ed. *Fukko wayō* (Revival of Japanese style). (*Nihon no sho* 11). Tokyo: Chūō Kōronsha, 1982.

———, ed. *Kan'ei sanpitsu* (The three brushes of Kan'ei [1624–1644]). (*Nihon no sho* 10). Tokyo: Chūō Kōronsha, 1981.

Kuboki Shōichi. *Kojima Sōshin wakakan* (A poetry scroll by Kojima Sōshin). (*Nihon meiseki sōkan* 27). Tokyo: Nigensha, 1979.

Nihon no sho (Japanese calligraphy). Tokyo: Tokyo National Museum, 1978.

Shimazaki Susumu. "Kanazawa chihō ni okeru Sōtatsu-ha—Sōsetsu to Sōsetsu ni tsuite" (The Sōtatsu school in Kanazawa—concerning the two Sōsetsu). In Yamane Yūzō, ed., *Sōtatsu-ha 2* (*Rinpa kaiga zenshū* 2). Tokyo: Nihon Keizai Shinbunsha, 1978.

Stenchecum, Amanda Mayer. *Kosode: 16th–19th Century Textiles from the Nomura Collection*. New York and Tokyo: Japan Society and Kodansha International, 1984.

Takeda Tsuneo. *Shōheiga* (Wall and screen painting). (*Zaigai Nihon no shihō* 4). Tokyo: Asahi Shinbunsha, 1979.

Tamamushi Satoko. "Kinsei shōki no byōbu to ryōshi sōshoku—Shōkadō Shōjō hitsu *Chokusenshū waka byōbu* o megutte—" (Early early-modern folding screens and decorated paper—focusing on the *Chokusenshū waka* screens by Shōkadō Shōjō). *Bijutsushi* 117 (March 1985): 55–75.

Tanaka Yūjirō, ed. *Hon'ami Kōetsu*. (*Shodō geijutsu* 18). Tokyo: Chūō Kōronsha, 1971.

Yamato bunka, no. 45 (August 1966). The entire issue is devoted to Hon'ami Kōetsu, and sixty-three poetry sheets are published.

Index

Underlined page numbers indicate location of illustrations.

Aburanokōji Takusada (1625–1699), 116
Aburanokōji Takatsune (1682–1746), 112
Akashi, 26
Arisugawa Yukihito (1655–1699), 110
Ariwara Motokata (late ninth, early tenth century), 117
Ariwara Narihira (ca. 825–880), 13–14, 54, 58, 62–63, 66, 67, 73, 74, 81
Asukai Masaaki (1610–1679), 116
Asukai Masatoyo (d. 1712), 110
Autumn Poem on Cherry Blossoms (Kōetsu and Sōtatsu), 14, 15, 86, 99
"Azusayumi" (*Tales of Ise*, episode 24), 61, 70, 71–73, 73

"Broken Wall" (*Tales of Ise*, episode 5), 58, 58, 60, 62, 70, 70, 74

chanoyu, 19–20, 93–94
Chaya Shirōjirō (seventeenth century), 116
chigusa Ariyoshi (1614–1687), 116, 117
chirashigaki, 38

Daigo Fuyumoto (d. 1697), 110
Deer Scroll (Kōetsu and Sōtatsu), 14, 14–15, 97, 98
Diary of Murasaki Shikibu, 44
Dōjō Hōshinnō, Imperial Prince (d. 1249), 27, 28
Dōkō, Prince of the Shōkō-in (1611–1679), 116

Egyō, Monk (late tenth century), 117
"Eight Bridges." *See* "Yatsuhashi"
"Emperor's Visit to Sumiyoshi" (*Tales of Ise*, episode 117), 67, 68

Famous-place painting. *See* meisho-e
"Flight along Akuta River" (*Tales of Ise*, episode 6), 58–59, 58–59, 60, 62
Flowering Cherry and Autumn Maple with Poem Slips (artist unknown), 15, 85, 104–5, 108
Flowering Cherry and Autumn Maple with Poem Slips (Mitsuoki), 15, 104–5, 108
"Former Mistress in Kawachi Province" (*Tales of Ise*, episode 23), 66, 66
Fubokushō (1310), 108
Fujimoto Ryōin (fl. 1698), 116
Fujiwara Atsutada (906–943), 116
Fujiwara Chikage (d. 929), 116
Fujiwara Genshi (994–1027), 117
Fujiwara Ietaka (1158–1237), 102, 115, 116

Genji monogatari. See Tale of Genji
Gojō Tameyasu (1618–1677), 116
Gomizunoo, Emperor (1596–1680), 37
Gosenshū (*Gosen wakashū*; mid-tenth century), 23
goshiki-bon, 57
Gotoba (1180–1239; emperor, 1183–1198; Gotoba'in, retired emperor, 1198–1239), 12, 20, 25, 26, 102, 108, 116, 117
Goyōzei, Emperor (1571–1617), 19, 19
Gyōjo, Tonsured Prince (1639–1695), 117

haiga, 53
Hamuro Yoritaka (1643–1709), 116
hikime kagibana, 62
Hino Hirosuke (d. 1687), 117
Hino Mitsuyoshi (1591–1630), 112
Hino Sukekatsu (1577–1639), 112
Hitomaro, 20
Hōin Ryōshu, 117
Hollyhocks and Clematis (Shōkadō), 88–89, 91–92, 99
Ho'nami Kōetsu (1558–1637), 13, 14, 14–15, 15, 51, 54, 84, 86, 87–91, 92–93, 94, 96–99, 106
honka, 44
honka dori, 22–23, 25, 28, 33, 80, 91
Horikawa (1078–1107; emperor, 1087–1107), 23, 116
Hosokawa Yūsai (1534–1610), 16, 18, 20, 22–23, 25, 27
Hyakunin isshu (One Hundred Poems by One Hundred Poets; comp. Teika), 18–19
hyakushu uta, 20n7, 25

Fujiwara Kanesue (1285–1339), 116
Fujiwara Kinmitsu (1130–1178), 116
Fujiwara Kintō (996–1041), 117
Fujiwara Kōshi (842–910), 54, 58
Fujiwara Morosane (1042–1101), 117
Fujiwara Nagakiyo (fl. 1310), 116
Fujiwara Mototoshi (?–1142 or 1143), 115
Fujiwara Nobuzane (1177–1265), 116
Fujiwara Okikaze (ninth century), 113, 116
Fujiwara Sadanobu (1088–1156), 87, 87
Fujiwara Sanemasa (1018–1093), 116
Fujiwara Shigetsune (Monk Soi, d. 1094), 117
Fujiwara Shunzei (Toshinari, 1114–1204), 23, 25, 117
Fujiwara Suketaka, 116
Fujiwara Tadamichi (1097–1164), 114
Fujiwara Takanobu (1142–1205), 116
Fujiwara Tameie (1198–1275), 116
Fujiwara Tamesuke (1263–1328), 117
Fujiwara Tameuji (1222–1286), 18n3
Fujiwara Teika (Sadaie, 1162–1241), 12–13, 18–20, 21, 22, 23, 25, 26, 27, 28, 48, 94–95, 102, 108, 116
Fujiwara Tsunehira (1005–1072), 117
Fujiwara Tsunehira (d. 1274), 25
Fujiwara Yorimune (993–1065), 114
fukasa, 22, 37
fukinuki yatai, 62
Furuta Oribe (d. 1615), 94

Imadegawa Koresue (1659–1709), 110
In no on'utaawase (Shigeyuki), 98–99, 102
Ise monogatari. See Tales of Ise
"Ise Virgin's Visit" (*Tales of Ise*, episode 69), 13, 54, 56, 57, 61, 62, 63, 66, 69, 70, 72, 73–74, 73
Iwakura Tomooki (1601–1660), 112
Iwasa Matabei (1578–1650), 54

Jiin, Tonsured Prince (d. 1699), 117
Jimyōin Mototoki (1634–1704), 110, 116
Jiteiki, 18, 22
Juntoku, Emperor (1197–1242), 116

Kaide Umenenosuke Tomoyasu, 80n3
Kaihō Yūsen, 48
Kakinomoto Hitomaro, (fl. seventh century), 20
Kakuen, Monk (twelfth century), 117
Kamo no Chōmei (1155?–1216), 88, 90, 91, 113
kana, 87–89, 91, 93
kanji, 89, 91
Kano Tan'yū (1602–1674), 25, 33, 34, 36, 37, 48, 48–49, 49, 50
Karasumaru Mitsuhiro (1579–1638), 16, 18, 19, 20, 22–23, 25, 27, 34n3, 58, 90, 91, 95, 96
Karasumaru Sukeyoshi (1621–1669), 117
kasen-e, 38, 53
Kawachi Province, 66
Kazan'in Mochishige, 110
Kenshu, Monk, 117
Kenshun, Monk (1299–1357), 117
Ki no Tsurayuki (ca. 872–945), 12, 16, 27, 99, 115, 116, 117
kirei sabi, 94
Kitano tenjin engi (Legend of Sugawara no Michizane), 76, 80
Kobori Enshū (1579–1647), 37, 94–95
Koga Michinari (1659–1719), 110
Kokinshū (*Kokin wakashū*; ca. 914–920), 16, 18, 54
Kojima Sōshin (1580–ca. 1655), 15, 94–95, 99
Kōken, Monk of the Sanbō-in, 116
Kokin denjū, 16, 18, 95
Konoe Nobuhiro (1599–1649), 102–3, 106
Konoe Nobutada (1565–1614), 84, 92, 96, 106
Konparu Zenchiku (1405–1468), 18n5
Kujō Kaneharu (1640–1677), 116, 117
Kujō Suzekane, (1668–1729), 110
Kumano Shrine, 25–26
Kuze Shigeyuki (1660–1720), 98–99, 102

Maigetsushō (Teika), 23
Man'yōgana, 49, 108
Man'yōshū (eighth century), 23, 26, 28
Meigetsuki (diary of Teika), 27–28, 102
meisho, 25
meisho-e, 13–14, 67, 70, 80, 83, 108
Mikohidari Tameshige (1325–1385), 117
Minamoto Kanemitsu (d. 966), 117
Minamoto Masakane (1079–1143), 116
Minamoto Michinari (d. 1019), 116
Minamoto Moroyori (1070–1139), 117
Minamoto Nobumitsu, 117

122 *Word in Flower*

Minamoto Shigeyuki (939?–1000), 117
Minamoto Toshiyori (?1055–1129), 116
Minamoto Tsunenobu (1016–1097), 116
Minamoto Yoshikata (d. after 1155), 116
Minase Shrine, 22
Motoori Norinaga (1730–1801), 53
"Mt. Fuji" (Tales of Ise, episode 9), 63, 64, 66–67, 68
"Mt. Utsu" (Tales of Ise, episode 9), 55, 63, 65, 70, 75–76, 77, 80
Musashi Plain, 14, 54, 83
"Musashi Plain" (Tales of Ise, episode 12), 81, 83, 103
Musashi Plain (artist unknown), 54, 80–81, 103

Nagaie (1005–1064), 117
Naga no Imiki Okimaro, 26
Nakanoin Michikatsu (1556–1610), 54
Nakanoin Michimochi (1630–1710), 116, 117
Nakanoin Michini (fl. 1690), 110
Nakazane, 116
Nishi Hongan-ji, 87
Nishinotōin Tokinari (1645–1724), 112
Niwata Shigeeda (1650–1725), 110
Nō theater, 18, 19
"Nunobiki Falls" (Tales of Ise, episode 87), 67, 70, 75, 76

Ōe Masafusa (1041–1111), 116
Ogata Kenzan (1663–1743), 33, 46–47, 48–50, 51, 53
Ogata Kōrin (1658–1716), 81
Ogata Sōken (1621–1687), 15, 96–97, 99, 102
Ōgimachi Kimimichi (1652–1733), 111
Ōinomikado Norimitsu (1637–1704), 116, 117
Ōnakatomi Yoshinobu (921–991), 113, 117

Pampas Grass and Bush Clover, 14, 100–101, 102, 103, 106
Poems from the Senzaishū (Sōshin), 99
Poems from the Tsurayuki-shū (Sadanobu), 87, 87
Poems on Flowers and Birds of the Twelve Months (Teika), 13, 27, 28–31, 33
Poppies (follower of Sōsetsu), 14, 100–101, 106
Portrait of Fujiwara Teika (artist unknown), 24, 94
Portrait of Fujiwara Teika (Tan'yū), 34

ranbu, 18, 23, 25
Reizei Tamesuke (1263–1328), 116
"Returning Waves" (Tales of Ise, episode 7), 58, 59, 59, 60, 62, 70, 71, 74–75
Rokujō Arifuji (1672–1729), 112
Ryōsen Hōshi, 116

"Sacred Fence" (Tales of Ise, episode 71), 70, 75, 75
Saga-bon (Saga edition), 13, 54, 56, 58, 62, 63, 84
Sagami (fl. ca. 1050), 116
Saigyō (1118–1190), 80
Saionji Saneharu (1618–1677), 116
Saishō Shitennōin (monastery in Kyoto), 26, 27

Sakanoe Korenori, 116
Sanjō Kintomi (1619–1677), 116
Sanjōnishi Kin'eda (1487–1563), 18n3
Sanjōnishi Saneki (1511–1579), 18n3, 23
Sanjōnishi Sanetaka (Shōyōin; 1455–1537), 18n3, 20
Sano Crossing (Sano no watari), 25–26
Sano Crossing (school of Sōtatsu), 17, 26, 29
Seikanji Hirosada (1661–1707), 117
Sengohyakuban utaawase, 20n7
Sen no Rikyū (1522–1591), 94
Senzaishū (Sōshin), 15, 94–95, 99
Shigi no hagaki (A fluttering of snipe's wings; 1691), 45, 48, 49
shikishi, 36, 38, 84, 87
Shimizudani Sanenari (fl. 1672), 110
Shinkei, Tonsured Prince of the Ichijō-in, 117
Shin kokinshū (*Shin kokin wakashū*; 1216), 18, 23, 28, 84, 87, 94, 96, 96–97, 98, 99, 108
Shinshō, Tonsured Prince (Priest Genshō; late fourteenth century), 117
Shirakawa (Shirakawa'in; Retired Emperor, 1053–1129), 87
Shōkadō Shōjō (1584–1639), 88–89, 91–93, 94, 96, 99
Shoku kokinshū (*Shoku kokin wakashū*; 1439), 25
Shokushi (Shikishi), Imperial Princess (d. 1201), 19, 116
Shōson, Tonsured Prince (1303–1370), 117
Shūigusō (Teika), 27
Shūishū (*Shūi wakashū*; ca. 1005–1011), 20
Shunshi (consort of Emperor Gohorikawa, 1212–1275), 27
Sōnai Kaneyasu (fl. 1207), 26, 27
Sonohara, 108
Sono Motofuku (1621–1699), 116
Sono Motokatsu (1662–1738), 117
Sōnsho, Tonsured Prince of the Shōren-'in, 116
Sosei, Monk (late tenth century), 117
Sosonji Yukiyoshi (1180–fl. 1249), 116
Spring Azaleas and Autumn Rushes (attrib. Nobuhiro), 102–3, 106
Sugawara no Michizane (845–903), 80
Suma, 26
"Sumida River" (Tales of Ise, episode 9), 63, 64, 66, 66
Suminokura Sōan (1571–1632), 13, 54, 84
Sumiyoshi Shrine, 14, 67, 68, 70, 74, 75
Sutoku, Retired Emperor (1119–1164), 116, 117

Tachibana Tamenaka (fl. 1082), 114
Taira no Masaie, 116
Takatsukasu Kanehiro (1648–1725), 110
Takeno Jōō (1502–1555), 36n4
Takenouchi Toshiharu (1611–1647), 112
Tale of Genji, 16, 23, 26, 102, 108
Tale of the Hōgen War, 80n3
Tales of Ise, 13, 18, 28, 54, 56, 58, 58–59, 60–61, 62, 63, 64, 65, 66, 66, 67, 67, 68, 69, 70, 70–71, 72, 72–73, 73, 74, 74, 75, 75, 76, 77, 78–79, 80, 81, 90, 95, 102
Tales of Saigyō, 76, 80
Tanabe Castle, 16

tanzaku, 63, 80
Tawaraya Sōsetsu (fl. 1639–1650), 106
Tawaraya Sōtatsu (fl. 1600–1640), 14, 14–15, 38n6, 55, 70–71, 74, 75, 76, 77, 84, 86, 87–91, 96–97, 106
Teika Poem Written on Poem Slip (attrib. Emperor Goyōzei), 19, 19
Teika's Poems on Flowers and Birds of the Twelve Months, 6, 13, 28, 32, 33–53, 35, 36, 39, 40–41, 42, 43, 45, 46–47, 48–49
Thirty-Six Immortal Poets, 54, 62, 87, 88, 93
Thirty-Six Immortal Poets (Narihara), 57, 62
Three Poems (Mitsuhiro), 91, 95
Tofukomon'in (Tokugawa Kazuko, 1606–1678), 99, 108, 116
Tokudaiji Kiminobu (1605–1684), 117
Tomohito, Prince (brother of Goyōzei), 16
Tominokōji Sanenori (1264–1349), 117
Tominokōji Yorinao (1612–1658), 117
Tosa Ittoku (fl. early seventeenth century), 70–71, 70–71, 72–73
Tosa Mitsunari (1646–1710), 36–37, 40–41, 42, 44, 48, 53
Tosa Mitsuoki (1617–1691), 15, 33, 35–37, 35, 44, 104–5, 108, 116
Tō Tsuneyori (1401–1494), 18n3
tsukinami, 27
Tsurayuki-shū, 87, 87, 89
Twelve Poems from the Shin kokinshū (Kōetsu), 14, 92–93, 98

utaawase, 20, 25

"Visit to Sumiyoshi" (Tales of Ise, episode 68), 70, 74, 75

waka, 18, 20, 22, 27, 37, 38
"Well Curb" (Tales of Ise, episode 23), 81
"Writing on Water" (Tales of Ise, episode 50), 69

Yamabe Akahito (eighth century), 117
Yamamoto Soken (fl. 1683–1706), 6, 15, 28, 32, 33, 35, 37–38, 39, 40–41, 43, 44–45, 48, 49, 53
Yamamoto Sotei (fl. late seventeenth century), 37
Yanagihara Sukeyuki (1619–1679), 117
Yatsuhashi, 13–14
"Yatsuhashi" ("Eight Bridges"; Tales of Ise, episode 9), 63, 65, 81
yōen, 22
Yoshida (district in Kyoto), 18
yūgen, 22
Yūgimon'in (1270–1307), 117

Zeami Motokiyo (1363–1443), 26
Zhang Ji-zhi (1186–1266), 98n10

Design, Greer Allen

Typesetting, Hoblitzelle Graphics

Printing, Eastern Press, Inc.

Binding, Mueller Trade Bindery

Production supervision, Yale University Printing Service

Illustrations:

Charles Altschul, *Map, p. 122*

Sheldan Comfert Collins, *Fig. 52 (cover)*

Sheldan Comfert Collins and Jim Strong, *Fig. 52*

Schecter Lee, *Figs. 2, 3, 10, 16, 18, 46*

Thor Moser, *Fig. 35*

Otto E. Nelson, *Figs. 8, 28, 41, 48, 54*

Robert D. Rubic, *Figs. 29, 30, 33, 36, 53*

Joseph Szaszfai, *Figs. 2, 3, 10, 16, 18, 46*